GALLOPING GOURMET®'S NEW WAY TO COOK BOOK

WITH THE KITCHEN APPLIANCE THAT'S SWEEPING THE NATION

The Cookbook for Countertop Convection Ovens

By Bob Warden

THE GALLOPING
GOURMET®

Copyright© 1993, Direct Innovative Products, Inc.
Galloping Gourmet® licensing rights granted by Intermax, Inc.
Printed and bound in the U.S.A.
Published by Direct Innovative Products, Inc.
1101 Market Street, Suite 1300
Philadelphia, Pennsylvania 19107
 3 4 5 6 7 8 9
Library of Congress Catalog Card Number in Process
ISBN 0-9635755-0-3

This book is dedicated to my daughter, Becky, who gave all the people she met the inspiration to do their best,

and to my other children, David, Rachel, Jonathan, Joseph and Michael, who are living her example.

Credits:

Dinnerware and Flatware
BLOOMINGDALE'S

Photography
STEPHEN BARTH

Food Stylist
LANI DEAN

Food Coordinator
GAIL MOROSKY

Designer
ROBERT MILLER

Illustrator
LEWIS LONG

Typography
JANET DODD
CHRIS CASSIDY

Copy Editor
LISA RALPH

TABLE OF CONTENTS

A SILVER ANNIVERSARY

Almost 25 years ago a title was being sought for a new television cooking show then under consideration. The show would feature an expert in the culinary arts who could demonstrate cooking techniques while providing entertaining and articulate commentary.

The name "Galloping Gourmet" was selected on the basis of the sound of the words together as well as the literal meaning. A sense of movement and motion, rhythm and power were suggested by the word "galloping." This was wedded to a sense of the enjoyment of food as expressed by "gourmet." The impact was strengthened by the alliteration of the "g's" in Galloping Gourmet. And even though the show and name proved to be a perfect fit, and the "Galloping Gourmet" became one of the most popular television shows here and abroad, no one predicted that the name would outlast the program and be around for a quarter of a century. The name "Galloping Gourmet" has evolved from the mere name of the television show to something that represents a lot more indeed.

It's a cliche, of course, but nonetheless true: Americans have a love affair with food. To be truly successful, the food preparation process must lead to great taste, a feeling of satisfaction from eating well, and good health, the *sine qua non* of life, which can only be derived from the use of high quality foods and the best kitchen aid products to prepare them.

It is now a matter of historical record that the name "Galloping Gourmet" is a symbol of an ongoing love affair with good food and good cooking, of good taste and of good quality for home cooks everywhere.

INTRODUCTION

Suppose there was a way to cook faster, better and healthier. And suppose food actually looked and tasted moister, more succulent, the way it does in fine restaurants. Now imagine that the way to achieve such fine culinary results was very inexpensive and extremely easy to use. Chefs and homeowners everywhere would want it. The method already exists: The Countertop Convection Oven.

In this, the first major book on Countertop Convection Oven cooking, you'll learn what brought about this kitchen revolution and how this way of cooking gained its current enormous popularity.

You'll see why Countertop Convection cooking is superior to conventional methods and how it provides healthier and more nutritious meals. I'll also give you some points to remember when planning to cook healthy meals in your Countertop Convection Oven.

Also included are some mealtime guidelines that I've found indispensable. They'll help you get the most out of your convection oven experience.

Finally, the main course, if you will: A collection of recipes that run the gamut from delectable appetizers to sumptuous entrees to sinfully delicious desserts. In all, nearly 200 recipes were developed especially for this book and are included for your dining pleasure.

America Has Found A New Way To Cook

The development of the Countertop Convection Oven is an example of the old story that all things can be improved over time. Who would have thought that there could be any new breakthroughs in ways of cooking food? But, just as science and technology have paved the way for advances in other aspects of our lives, they have led to the development of new and better kitchen products. Our cooking tools have changed as the way we eat has changed. We've taken great steps toward healthier eating and now, by using the Countertop Convection Oven, healthier cooking is within our grasp.

For over 40 years, the Convection Oven has been an integral part of restaurant kitchens and bakeries. The ability of these ovens to provide better cooking results has made them essential to the food service industry. Just over a decade ago, the first convection ovens became available for home use. Initially, the idea was heartily welcomed. But it wasn't until the introduction of the round, countertop models that wide acceptance for home use was achieved. The round shape is not only more convenient for storage and handling, but also allows the hot air to circulate more efficiently. These improved appliances have found a place in kitchens all across the country.

As Seen On TV

In large part, the Countertop Convection Oven owes its wide acceptance and popularity to television. With the help of programs demonstrating the virtues of this cooking marvel we learned just how easy it is to create culinary delights faster than ever before. And, because we've seen it done, we've become comfortable using this uncomplicated kitchen appliance. For these reasons, people all across the country have fallen in love with the Countertop Convection Oven in a very big way.

Television was the informative tool that worked wonders to communicate the simple laws of physics these ovens apply. People saw head-to-head cooking comparisons between convection ovens and conventional ovens. They saw breads rise dramatically higher, fish and poultry cooked evenly to perfection and vegetables steamed to succulence with no loss of flavor or nutrients. And it was all done faster and easier with the modern Countertop Convection Oven. In the end, there was no comparison. Virtually overnight we learned how this new kitchen appliance answered our need as a culture to provide a better way of cooking for ourselves and our families.

WHY CONVECTION COOKING IS BETTER

Traditional methods of cooking have some inherent limitations. In the conventional oven and on the stove heat radiates upwards. Foods close to the heat source cook faster while foods further away cook slower. Anyone who's spent time in the kitchen knows about the problems of unevenly cooked foods and the constant monitoring required to ensure acceptable results.

On the other hand, Convection Ovens employ a fan inside to circulate the heat. You don't need to turn kabobs or flip burgers in a modern Countertop Convection Oven to get the results you want. The secret is the oven's circular shape that allows air to move freely. The better the air flow, the more evenly and faster it cooks. Reduced cooking time also results in substantial energy savings.

A key benefit of the product is the quick searing provided by the oven's hot air. You can actually cook different types of food at the same time without the blending of flavors, as I do on TV and at home. If the kids want hamburgers and my wife and I want fish, we cook them side by side with results that make everybody happy.

THE REAL BENEFITS ARE TASTE, HEALTH AND CONVENIENCE

Now it is possible to achieve the taste of fine restaurant cooking at home. Meats are moist and tender with very little shrinkage. Baked goods brown evenly, rise higher and have the look of professionally prepared foods.

The nature of the Countertop Convection Oven also allows you to prepare complete meals at one time. And, as long as the foods are not touching the sides, the flow of heated air circulates in and around to give incredibly fast results.

Foods placed directly on the racks cook quickest. The hot air rapidly seals in the natural juices while excess fat and calories drip away.

Until I began using the Countertop Convection Oven, I never believed you could cook healthier and achieve better-tasting foods. Believe me, you can. Just take a look at the recipes in this book. Each one gives you a simple way to create extraordinary cuisine on an everyday basis.

I DID IT ON TV, YOU CAN DO IT AT HOME

Some of us are natural experimenters, others are reluctant to try new methods of cooking. To the hesitant, I say that everything I've done with the Countertop Convection

Oven on TV you can easily do at home. Start with one of the many recipes in this book. Then try experimenting with an old family favorite. Using your tried and true recipes, your eyes and your mouth, you'll quickly achieve new taste-tempting results.

Now, suppose someone told you there was a way to cook faster, better and healthier than ever before. Would you want to try it? And suppose there were mouth-watering recipes for food that actually tasted the way it does in fine restaurants. Would you want to cook food that way? Of course you would.

GUIDELINES FOR GREAT EATING

Just as there are fads in fashion, there are fads in how we think about food, too. Fortunately, modern science allows us to make more informed decisions about food. There are many new ways to think about our cooking methods and eating habits. By focusing on the most important ones, we'll see how to eat healthier, more satisfying meals.

■ Think about appropriate portions. Many of us learned to clean our plates and couldn't leave the table until we did so. Now, heaping helpings are a thing of the past. Health professionals advise us to reduce caloric intake by eating less, an important factor in lifelong good health. More and more, people are eating lighter, healthier meals without diminishing the enjoyment of food.

■ Don't be confined to the traditional meal landscape: appetizer, soup, salad, entree, dessert. A meal can be whatever you want it to be. You can take a full portion of an appetizer or soup and make it a meal. If it's healthy and delicious, you can't go wrong.

■ Food today is being prepared in more interesting combinations - traditional meals are changing. Be creative; substitute an interesting rice or spicy vegetable dish for a baked potato. Try a new fish or poultry dish instead of beef. Excursions into unknown culinary territory are fun and rewarding.

■ Try different flavors. Take a favorite dish and give it a twist with a new type of seasoning. The American palate is attuned to salt and pepper, but other cultures have used different and exotic spices for centuries. Bear in mind that herbs have a shelf life of approximately six months. For the best results, always make sure your herbs and spices are fresh.

■ Many foods that were once considered taboo are now widely accepted as healthy. We now see the value of breads, potatoes and pastas, things that many health-conscious people crossed off their lists long ago. Similarly, vegetarian dishes have gained a well-deserved popularity and are increasingly served as a main course, not only as a side dish. In the past, meals were built around a main course of meat. Side dishes were an afterthought chosen from what was available in the pantry. Now pasta, vegetables and other nutritious entrees are challenging meat as the standard main course.

■ Fresh is the focus. Many people can remember when oranges were so rare they were given as gifts during the winter months. Now there is a huge variety of fresh fruits and vegetables available all year round. Take advantage of the bounty available at your supermarket or grocer's by choosing fresh produce over frozen or canned offerings.

■ Try something different when you entertain. You don't have to set the table in the traditional arrangement. Try a buffet in a different room or create an atmosphere that complements the meal you are preparing.

GETTING THE MOST OUT OF YOUR COUNTERTOP CONVECTION OVEN

Below you'll find some simple tips to remember when you cook with a Countertop Convection Oven. By utilizing these techniques you can ensure the finest results and count on an enjoyable cooking experience.

1. Most pans can be used in your Countertop Convection Oven.

Metal pans do best but there's no reason to throw away your glass bowls. As a matter of fact, many of the recipes in this book were cooked using a glass pan - the same kind found in most kitchens.

2. Different pans give different results.

In Convection Ovens, as with conventional ovens, different types of cooking pans will give different results. For instance, dark and dull metal pans or dark non-stick pans are recommended for crispier results and darker crusts. Light and shiny metal pans will give you lighter, more tender crusts.

3. Food should be placed where circulating air can get to it.

Large roasts that touch the side of the cooking bowl will require turning during cooking. Try to avoid any portion of the food touching the side so that you can achieve faster, more even cooking without the extra handling.

4. No need to rotate the kabobs.

With high speed air circulating throughout the oven your foods cook evenly on all sides, so there's no need to rotate the foods you cook unless your foods are too close together or touch the sides of the bowl.

5. Upper Rack vs. Lower Rack

While most of the recipes in this book suggest you use the lower cooking rack, that does not mean you can't cook on the upper rack as well. As a matter of fact, you can use any number of racks to achieve great results. Just be sure that foods don't touch and are kept away from the oven's heating element. Check your owner's manual for specific information about how close to the oven's heating element you can cook.

6. Lighter toppings may blow around.

The air circulating in your Countertop Convection Oven may make lighter toppings blow around. Until they melt or are blended in, you may have to cover them with a rack or aluminum foil. Once melted or set you can remove the cover.

7. You're not limited to this book's recipes.

Once you begin cooking with your Countertop Convection Oven, you'll discover many new ways to use it. Frozen foods, for instance, will come out tasting much better than if you were using a microwave oven. And, they'll cook faster than if you used a conventional oven. Give it a try.

8. Be careful - It's Hot!

Recipes in which the juices are seared or sealed inside will tend to be very hot when eaten right out of the oven. Foods like frozen hors d'oeuvres will rise higher and cook quickly, but be careful when you bite into them. They will be extremely hot to the touch and even hotter in the mouth.

9. When cooking complete meals together, remember this...

As most cooks already know, certain foods take longer than others to cook. Just select the foods that take the longest and start them ahead of the rest. That way all of your foods will be done perfectly and ready for eating when you are.

BEFORE YOU COOK

As with all cooking appliances, preheat time as well as cooking and baking time may vary by model and manufacturer. It is important to read the owner's manual of all appliances before using them.

Keep your Countertop Convection Oven and all electrical appliances out of reach of small children.

Veggie Wedgies-
Cheddar Cheese and
Broccoli on
English Muffin, *p.36*

Top:
Spinach Basil
Turnovers, p.30

Bottom:
Peppers Provencal, p.32

Top:
**Tiny New Potatoes
with Smoked Salmon,** *p.30*
Bottom:
**Crab and Brie
Tostadas with Fresh
Cranberry Salsa,** *p.34*

APPETIZERS AND PARTY FOODS

Company's coming. What should I serve?

Does that sound familiar? If the answer is yes, then you will probably find the solution in this and the following sections. Under Appetizers and Party Foods you'll discover tantalizing recipes that not only sound great, but also taste great.

If you'd like to serve something a little spicy with a Mexican flair, try the *Tortilla Pizza with Cheese, Chilies and Enchilada Sauce.* There's also a *Hot Mexicana Dip* that will send your taste buds South of the Border.

Maybe you'd like to serve something a little more reserved, such as the *Mini Southern Crab Cakes with Caper Tartar Sauce* or the *Tiny Herb Biscuits with Chive Spread and Roast Beef.* They're all recipes that are easy to prepare. You can make them quickly using your Countertop Convection Oven.

Start with something familiar, then work your way to something you haven't tried before. Be daring.

HOT AND SMOKY CHICKEN WINGS

Marinate: 8 hours or overnight
Cooking time: 18 minutes

3 pounds chicken wings
(about 16)

Marinade:
½ cup soy sauce
¼ cup peanut oil
¼ cup water
2 tablespoons Thai Chili paste *
1 tablespoon Oriental sesame oil
2 teaspoons liquid smoke

- Rinse chicken and pat dry. Cut off and discard wing tips. Cut each wing at joint to make 2 sections.

- Combine all the marinade ingredients in a large mixing bowl. Add the wings and toss to coat with marinade. Cover and marinate in the refrigerator for at least 8 hours or overnight.

- Place lower wire rack into bowl of oven. Preheat oven to 500°F.

- Remove chicken wings from marinade. Lay half the chicken wings on the lower rack. Put upper rack in place. Lay the remainder of wings on the upper rack.

- Reduce oven heat to 450°F. Cook wings for 10 minutes. Reduce oven heat to 400°F and continue cooking 5 minutes.

- Remove upper rack of wings. Keep warm. Continue cooking lower rack of wings for 3 more minutes. Serve while hot with hot sauce if desired.

   *Available at Oriental grocery stores and some supermarkets.

MINI OPEN FACE REUBENS

Cooking time: 4 minutes

½ pound corned beef, thinly sliced
½ pound Swiss cheese, thinly sliced
1 loaf cocktail rye bread
1 cup prepared Russian dressing
1½ cups sauerkraut

- Place upper wire rack into bowl of oven. Preheat oven to 500°F.

- Cut each slice of corned beef in half and cut each slice of cheese in quarters.

- Toast bread 10 to 12 slices at a time at 500°F for 1 to 2 minutes.
- Spread each piece of bread with 1 teaspoon Russian dressing. Top each toasted bread slice with half a slice of corned beef, a heaping teaspoon of sauerkraut and a ¼ slice of cheese on top.
- Cook the reubens at 500°F for 1 to 2 minutes or until cheese is melted and bubbly. Serve hot.

NACHOS SUPREME

Makes 8 Servings

Cooking time: 4 to 5 minutes

2 cups tortilla chips
1½ cups grated Monterey Jack cheese
1 cup canned black beans, drained and rinsed
¼ cup sliced pickled jalapeno peppers
¼ cup chopped black olives
1 cup prepared salsa
1 cup sour cream

- Place wire rack into bowl of oven. Preheat oven to 500°F.
- Spread tortilla chips on bottom of a 9-inch metal baking pan. Top with half the grated cheese. Sprinkle with black beans, jalapeno peppers and olives. Top with remainder of cheese.
- Reduce oven heat to 375°F. Bake nachos 4 to 5 minutes or until cheese is melted and all ingredients are hot. Serve immediately with dishes of salsa and sour cream.

HAVING LIVED IN THE WEST MOST OF MY LIFE, I'VE COME TO LOVE THE FOODS OF MEXICO. WITH MY TRAVEL SCHEDULE, I HAVE FOUND THAT THE ENTIRE COUNTRY FEELS THE SAME WAY. THE RECIPE ABOVE FOR NACHOS SUPREME IS JUST ONE OF THE MANY MEXICAN INSPIRED RECIPES YOU WILL FIND IN THIS BOOK.

✔ *Check your owner's manual for preheating time which may vary by manufacturer.*

HAM AND CHEESE BISCUITS WITH MUSTARD MAYO

Makes 20

Cooking time: 10 to 12 minutes

*1½ cups buttermilk baking mix
(such as Bisquick)*
⅓ cup minced ham
⅓ cup finely grated Swiss cheese
½ cup milk

Mustard Mayo:
⅓ cup mayonnaise
1½ tablespoons grainy mustard

- Place wire rack into bowl of oven. Preheat oven to 500°F.

- Grease two 9-inch metal baking pans.

- Combine baking mix, ham and cheese. Toss with fingers to mix well, coating ham and cheese with mix. Add milk. Mix with hands to incorporate all ingredients and form a soft dough.

- Turn dough out onto a floured surface. Knead 10 times. Pat dough to ¾-inch thickness. With a 1½-inch cutter make 20 biscuit shapes, reforming scraps and using all the dough.

- Place 10 biscuits in each pan. Reduce oven heat to 425°F. Bake for 10 to 12 minutes or until nicely browned. Repeat with remaining biscuits. Cool on wire rack.

- While biscuits are cooling, mix mayonnaise and mustard in small bowl until smooth. When cool, spread biscuits with mustard mayo.

ARTICHOKE AND SCALLION GRATIN

Makes 8 Servings

Cooking time: 20 minutes

1 cup scallions, chopped
1 cup mayonnaise
½ cup sour cream
2½ tablespoons grated Romano cheese
2½ tablespoons grated Parmesan cheese
10-ounces artichoke hearts packed in water

- Place wire rack into bowl of oven. Preheat oven to 500°F.

- In a small bowl combine the scallions, mayonnaise, sour cream and cheeses. Break up the artichoke hearts (separate the leaves) and scatter them on the bottom of an 8-inch glass pie plate or au gratin dish. Pour the mayonnaise mixture over the artichoke hearts.

- Place a piece of aluminum foil the same size as baking dish directly on wire rack. Place dish on foil.

- Reduce oven heat to 350°F. Bake 20 minutes or until hot, bubbly and browned on top. Serve warm with crackers.

SESAME SCALLION CHICKEN BITES

Makes 30 to 35

Cooking time: 10 to 12 minutes

2 pounds skinless, boneless chicken breasts
2 cups buttermilk baking mix (such as Bisquick)
½ cup minced scallions
3 tablespoons sesame seeds
1 teaspoon ground ginger
2 teaspoons garlic powder
2 eggs, well beaten
1 tablespoon Oriental sesame oil

- Place lower wire rack into bowl of oven. Preheat oven to 500°F.

- Cut chicken into 1-inch square pieces.

- Combine baking mix, scallions, sesame seeds, ginger and garlic powder in a shallow bowl. In a separate bowl, mix eggs and sesame oil.

- Coat chicken pieces in egg mixture, then roll in biscuit mix mixture, coating well.

- Reduce oven heat to 400°F. Place about 15 chicken pieces in each of two 9-inch metal baking pans. Bake one pan at a time 10 to 12 minutes or until golden brown. Serve hot.

HOT AND CREAMY CRAB DIP

Makes 2 Cups

Cooking time: 15 minutes

8-ounces fresh crabmeat
8-ounces cream cheese, softened
½ cup mayonnaise
1 teaspoon Worcestershire sauce
2 tablespoons red pepper, finely chopped
2 tablespoons scallions, finely chopped

- Place wire rack into bowl of oven. Preheat oven to 500°F.
- Check that crabmeat is free of shells and cartilage.
- In mixer bowl or food processor, combine cream cheese, mayonnaise and Worcestershire sauce until well blended. Add red pepper and scallions. Mix with a spoon until just combined. Gently fold in crabmeat.
- Pour dip into a 6x6-inch ovenproof dish. Cover tightly with foil. If using glass or ceramic dish, place a piece of foil the same size as the baking dish directly on the wire rack. Place baking dish on top of foil.
- Reduce oven heat to 350°F. Bake for 15 minutes or until hot. Serve hot with crackers or crudités.

BACON, TOMATO AND CHEESE TURNOVERS

Makes 45

Cooking time: 10 minutes

1½ cups grated Cheddar cheese
6 strips bacon, cooked and crumbled
½ cup crushed tomatoes
3 sheets prepared pie crust dough

- Place wire rack into bowl of oven. Preheat oven to 500°F.
- Place cheese and bacon in food processor. Process until bacon is very finely chopped. Add tomatoes. Pulse once or twice to combine.
- With 3-inch biscuit cutter or rim of a drinking glass, cut circles of pie dough. Re-roll scraps and cut again. Each sheet of dough should yield 15 circles.

- Place a teaspoon of filling in the center of each 3-inch circle. Fold edge over to form a semi-circle. Press edges firmly with tines of a fork to seal. Prick once with fork to form steam vents. Arrange turnovers in a 9-inch metal baking pan.

- Reduce oven heat to 375°F and bake for 10 minutes or until lightly browned. Repeat with remaining dough. Serve hot.

SURPRISE STUFFED MUSHROOMS

Makes 16

Cooking time: 10 to 12 minutes

16 medium sized mushrooms
16 scallops
1 tablespoon olive oil
1 tablespoon butter
2 cloves garlic, minced
2 tablespoons fresh parsley, chopped
1 tablespoon fresh lemon juice
Salt and pepper to taste
½ cup Gruyére cheese, grated

- Wash and drain mushrooms. Remove stems.

- Rinse scallops, removing any shell pieces. Halve any large scallops. In a medium frying pan, heat oil and butter together until bubbly. Add garlic and saute for 1 minute. Add scallops and saute 1 to 3 minutes or until they become opaque. Add parsley, lemon juice, salt and pepper. With slotted spoon, remove scallops to a dish. Reduce remaining juices in pan to a teaspoon. Return scallops to pan and toss with reduced juices.

- Place wire rack into bowl of oven. Preheat oven to 500°F.

- Arrange mushrooms cavity side up in a 9-inch metal baking pan. Fill each cavity with a scallop. Top with small amount of Gruyére. Cover pan tightly with foil.

- Reduce oven heat to 400°F. Bake mushrooms for 10 minutes. Uncover and continue baking for 2 minutes or until cheese begins to brown. Serve hot.

Tortilla Pizza with Cheese, Chilies and Enchilada Sauce

Cooking time: 5 minutes

3   6-inch corn tortillas
3-ounces Monterey Jack cheese, sliced into 9 small pieces
4-ounce can whole green chilies, sliced
6 tablespoons canned enchilada sauce

- Place wire rack into bowl of oven. Preheat oven to 500°F.

- Cut a 14x9-inch sheet of heavy duty aluminum foil. Fold in half to create a piece 7x9-inches. Place one tortilla on foil. Top with 3 cheese slices, ⅓ of the sliced chilies and 2 tablespoons of sauce.

- Reduce oven heat to 400°F. Place foil piece holding tortilla on oven rack. Bake 5 minutes. Remove carefully. Repeat steps two and three with remaining tortillas. Serve immediately.

Dried Beef and Onion Dip

Makes 2 Cups

Cooking time: 15 to 20 minutes

8-ounces cream cheese, softened
4-ounces sharp Cheddar cheese, grated
½ cup milk
¼ cup onion, finely chopped
4-ounces chipped dried beef

- Place wire rack into bowl of oven. Preheat oven to 500°F.

- Combine cream cheese, cheddar cheese, milk and onion in a mixer bowl or processor. Beat or process until well blended. Stir in dried beef.

- Turn dip into a small ovenproof dish (about 6x6-inches). Cover tightly with foil. If using glass or ceramic dish, place a piece of foil the same size as the dish directly on the wire rack and place the baking dish on the foil.

- Reduce oven heat to 350°F. Bake for 15 to 20 minutes or until hot. Serve hot with crackers or crudités.

Mini Southern Crab Cakes with Caper Tartar Sauce

Makes 24

Cooking time: 12 to 15 minutes

Caper Tartar Sauce:
½ cup mayonnaise
¼ cup capers
¼ cup chopped scallions
2 tablespoons lime juice
2 teaspoons hot sauce

1 pound fresh crabmeat
1 cup dry breadcrumbs
⅓ cup chopped scallions
⅓ cup chopped fresh parsley
½ cup mayonnaise
1 tablespoon Dijon mustard
½ cup melted butter

- Combine all the tartar sauce ingredients in a small bowl. Refrigerate until ready to use.
- Place lower wire rack into bowl of oven. Preheat oven to 500°F.
- Check that the crabmeat is free of shells and cartilage.
- Gently combine crabmeat, ¼ cup of the breadcrumbs, scallions, parsley, mayonnaise and mustard. Shape into about 24 small cakes. Spread remaining breadcrumbs on a plate and roll each cake with crumbs to coat.
- Lay 12 cakes directly on the lower rack, drizzle with half the butter. Place the upper rack in position. Lay the remaining cakes on the upper rack and drizzle with remaining butter.
- Reduce oven heat to 375°F. Bake 12 to 15 minutes or until browned and crusty. Serve on toothpicks with tartar sauce.

Tiny New Potatoes
with Smoked Salmon

Cooking time: 25 to 30 minutes

20 unblemished new red potatoes (you may select any small, thin skinned potato), about 1½-inches in diameter, scrubbed and dried

2 tablespoons sour cream, light sour cream, or plain yogurt

8-ounces cream cheese and smoked salmon spread

2 tablespoons prepared horseradish

- Place wire rack into bowl of oven. Preheat oven to 500°F.

- Reduce oven heat to 425°F. Place potatoes directly on wire rack. Bake for 25 minutes or until easily pierced with a fork. Remove and cool.

- Cut each potato in half crosswise. Scoop out pulp leaving ¼-inch thick shells. In a small bowl combine potato pulp and sour cream. Beat with an electric mixer until smooth. Add cream cheese spread and horseradish. Beat until smooth and fluffy.

- Fill each potato skin with some of the mixture. This is easily done with a spoon but you may want to use a pastry bag fitted with a decorative tip.

- Preheat oven to 500°F. Arrange about 10 potato halves in each of several 9-inch metal baking pans. Reduce oven heat to 425°F. Bake, one pan at a time, for 3 to 5 minutes or until browned and heated through. Allow to cool slightly before serving.

Spinach Basil Turnovers

Makes 30

Cooking time: 10 minutes

10-ounce package frozen spinach, thawed and squeezed dry

1 cup packed fresh basil leaves

3-ounces cream cheese

2 tablespoons dried (instant minced) onion rehydrated in 2 tablespoons water

Salt and pepper to taste

2 sheets prepared pie crust dough

- In bowl of food processor, process spinach, basil, cream cheese, onion, salt and pepper until blended.

- Place wire rack into bowl of oven. Preheat oven to 500°F.

- With a 3-inch biscuit cutter or rim of a drinking glass, cut circles of pie dough. Re-roll scraps and cut again. Each sheet of dough should yield 15 circles.

- Place a teaspoon of filling on each round, fold over to form a semi-circle. Press edges firmly with tines of fork to seal. Prick once with fork to form steam vents. Arrange turnovers in a 9-inch metal baking pan.

- Reduce oven heat to 375°F and bake for 10 minutes or until lightly browned. Repeat with remaining turnovers.

BAKED FRITTATA WITH GOLD POTATOES, RED ONIONS AND BLACK CAVIAR

Makes 6 Servings

Cooking time: 24 minutes

1 tablespoon olive oil

2 medium Yukon Gold potatoes or all-purpose potatoes, cut into ½-inch dice

1 large red onion, sliced very thin and cut into ½-inch pieces

Salt and pepper to taste

6 large eggs, well beaten

6 tablespoons sour cream

6 teaspoons black caviar

- Place wire rack into bowl of oven. Preheat oven to 500°F.

- Place olive oil in 9-inch metal baking pan. Toss potatoes and onion in oiled pan. Sprinkle with salt and pepper.

- Reduce oven heat to 400°F. Cook 15 minutes, stirring every 5 minutes.

- Pour beaten eggs over potatoes and onions. Reduce oven heat to 300°F and continue cooking for 8 minutes or until eggs are almost set. Raise heat to 500°F and broil frittata 1 minute.

- Cut into 6 wedges and top each with 1 tablespoon sour cream and 1 teaspoon caviar. Serve hot.

Peppers Provencal

Makes 2 Cups

Cooking time: 6 to 8 minutes

1 large green bell pepper

1 large red bell pepper

2 tablespoons olive oil

*¼ cup chopped black olives,
preferably nicoise*

2 teaspoons red wine vinegar

2 teaspoons balsamic vinegar

1 teaspoon garlic, minced

*1 tablespoon chopped fresh basil or
1 teaspoon dry basil*

½ teaspoon coarse or regular salt

½ teaspoon coarse ground black pepper

- Place wire rack into bowl of oven. Preheat oven to 500°F.

- Wash, seed and core peppers. Cut into ½-inch wide strips.

- Place 1 tablespoon of the oil in a 9-inch metal baking pan. Toss peppers in oil to coat.

- Reduce oven heat to 400°F. Put pan on rack and roast peppers for 6 to 8 minutes. Stir every few minutes, until tender and slightly charred.

- Place cooked peppers in a glass serving dish or platter. Drizzle with remaining oil, olives, vinegars, garlic, basil, salt and pepper. Toss to coat. Store covered in refrigerator. Bring to room temperature and serve with French or Italian bread.

Hot Mexicana Dip

Makes 3 Cups

Cooking time: 8 to 10 minutes

8-ounces cream cheese, room temperature

2 cups grated Monterey Jack cheese or Cheddar cheese

1 tablespoon lime juice

2 teaspoons hot sauce

1 teaspoon ground cumin

1½ cups prepared hot salsa

- Place wire rack into bowl of oven. Preheat oven to 500°F.

- Place the cheeses, lime juice, hot sauce and cumin in the work bowl of a food processor and process for 30 seconds. Add the salsa and process until just combined.

- Transfer dip to ovenproof 3-cup baking dish. If using a non-metal baking dish place a square of aluminum foil the same size as the dish directly on the wire rack. Set the dish on top of the foil.

- Reduce oven heat to 450°F. Bake for 8 to 10 minutes or until hot and bubbly. Serve with tortilla chips.

TINY HERB BISCUITS WITH CHIVE SPREAD AND ROAST BEEF

Makes 20

Cooking time: 10 to 12 minutes

1½ cups buttermilk baking mix (such as Bisquick)
1½ tablespoons fresh chopped sage, parsley or basil or a combination of the three
½ cup water
6-ounces cream cheese and chive spread
⅓ pound rare roast beef, thinly sliced

- Place wire rack into bowl of oven. Preheat oven to 500°F.

- Grease two 9-inch metal baking pans.

- In a medium bowl combine baking mix with herbs. Add water. Mix with hands until ingredients are well incorporated and a soft dough is formed.

- Turn dough out onto floured surface and knead 10 times. Pat dough to ¾-inch thickness. With a 1½-inch cutter make 20 biscuit shapes. Place 10 biscuits in each pan.

- Reduce oven heat to 425°F. Bake biscuits for 10 to 12 minutes or until lightly browned. Repeat with remaining biscuits. Cool on wire racks.

- Split each biscuit and spread both halves with a small amount of chive spread. Top one half with half a slice of roast beef. Put biscuit halves together to form a sandwich.

CRAB AND BRIE TOSTADAS WITH FRESH CRANBERRY SALSA

Cooking time: 3 to 5 minutes

Salsa:
1 cup fresh cranberries
¼ of a large orange
1 ½ tablespoons sugar

3 8-inch flour tortillas
5-ounces fresh crabmeat
6-ounces Brie, cut into bits

- Combine all salsa ingredients in the work bowl of a food processor. Process 30 seconds or until chopped fine. Set aside.
- Place wire rack into bowl of oven. Preheat oven to 500°F.
- Check that the crabmeat is free of shells and cartilage.
- Place one flour tortilla into a 9-inch metal baking pan. Top with 1½-ounces crabmeat and 2-ounces Brie.
- Reduce oven heat to 400°F. Bake tostada for 3 to 5 minutes or until cheese is melted and bubbly. Repeat with remaining tortillas. Allow each tostada to cool slightly. Cut into 6 wedges and serve with salsa.

CROSTINI WITH PEPPERONI AND PROVOLONE

Cooking time: 1 to 2 minutes

2 tablespoons olive oil
2 teaspoons garlic, minced
12 ½-inch thick slices French or Italian bread
24 thin slices of regular pepperoni
(or 12 slices of the larger variety)
12 slices smoked provolone cheese

- Place upper wire rack into bowl of oven. Preheat oven to 500°F.
- Combine oil and garlic in a small dish. Allow to stand several minutes.
- Brush one side of each bread slice with garlic/oil.
- Place as many slices as will fit directly on wire rack. Reduce oven heat to 450°F. Bake about 1 minute. Top with 2 slices of pepperoni and 1 slice of cheese and continue baking until cheese is melted, about 1 minute. Serve hot.

LEMONY RICE STUFFED GRAPE LEAVES

Makes 30

Cooking time: 15 minutes

30 canned grape leaves

1 cup long grain rice
(2½ cups cooked)

6 tablespoons olive oil

1 medium onion, chopped

1 tablespoon garlic, minced

2 teaspoons ground cumin

2 teaspoons instant chicken
broth granules

½ cup currants

⅓ cup toasted pine nuts

Grated rind of 2 lemons

½ cup finely chopped fresh mint
or parsley

Salt and pepper to taste

1 cup hot water

2 tablespoons fresh lemon juice

- Drop pale-green grape leaves into water to cover. Allow to soak 30 minutes.

- Cook and drain rice.

- Heat 3 tablespoons olive oil in a large frying pan. Add onion and garlic and saute until tender. Add cooked rice, cumin and 1 teaspoon chicken broth granules. Stir to combine. Mix in currants, nuts, rind and mint or parsley. Season with salt and pepper.

- Place wire rack into bowl of oven. Preheat oven to 500°F.

- Drain grape leaves. Arrange leaves, veined side up, on a work surface. Place 1 tablespoon filling on each stem end. Fold 2 short sides over filling, then roll up starting at stem end.

- Place about 15 stuffed leaves (loose side down) in a 9-inch nonstick coated metal baking pan. Combine water, lemon juice, remaining chicken broth granules and remaining olive oil. Pour half over grape leaves.

- Reduce oven heat to 400°F. Cover pan tightly with foil. Bake leaves for 15 minutes or until hot. Repeat with remaining leaves. Cool, then chill. Serve cold or at room temperature.

THE ABOVE RECIPE USES LONG GRAIN RICE, WHICH REMAINS SEPARATE AND FLUFFY WHEN COOKED. RICE IS EXTREMELY LOW IN FAT, HAS NO CHOLESTEROL AND IS A GREAT SOURCE OF COMPLEX CARBOHYDRATES.

Veggie Wedgies

Makes 48

Cooking time: 6 minutes

1 cup Cheddar cheese, grated or shredded
⅓ cup mayonnaise
¾ cup frozen chopped broccoli, thawed and drained
6 English muffins, split
Pimiento strips for garnish

- Place upper rack into bowl of oven. Preheat oven to 500°F.

- In a small bowl combine the cheese, mayonnaise and broccoli.

- Place 4 muffin halves on upper rack of oven. Reduce oven heat to 475°F. Cook until lightly toasted, about 3 minutes. Repeat with remaining muffins.

- Lay muffins on a work surface. Spread each half with some of the broccoli mixture. Garnish with pimento strips as desired. Return muffins, 3 or 4 at a time, to the upper rack. Grill 2 to 3 minutes or until hot and bubbly. Cut each into 4 wedges. Serve hot.

BROCCOLI IS ONE OF THE HEALTHIEST FOODS YOU CAN EAT. TODAY, FRESH BROCCOLI IS AVAILABLE YEAR ROUND. IT'S WELL KNOWN AS A FAVORITE SIDE DISH AND HAS A MAJOR ROLE AS A PARTY APPETIZER WHEN SERVED WITH OTHER UNCOOKED VEGETABLES. TRY IT WITH CRAB, HONEY-MUSTARD OR SOUR CREAM AND ONION DIPS.

BREADS, ROLLS & PIZZA

In Basket: (left to right)
Dark Beer Raisin Pumpernickel, *p.49;*
Mid-West Harvest Bread, *p.4*
Rosemary and Sun-Dried Tomato Focaccia, *p.47;*
Wonderful White Bread, *p.43*
Cutting Board:
Mid-West Harvest Bread, *p.46*

Basket:
Easy Pecan Pumpkin Muffins, p.45
Cape Cod Cranberry
Whole Wheat Muffins, p.44
Glass and Ivy Plates:
Orange Raisin Scones, p.61

Round Board (left):
Tuscan Black Pepper Bread, *p.48*

Round Board (right):
Braided Bagel Bread, *p.64*

Cutting Board (left):
Dark Beer Raisin Pumpernickel, *p.49*

Cutting Board (right):
Wonderful White Bread, *p.43*

BREADS, ROLLS AND PIZZA

Cuban Bread sounds unique and different - and it is. It bakes to perfection in your Countertop Convection Oven. Maybe you'd like to try something European, like *French Peasant Bread* or *Tuscan Black Pepper Bread* or even *Rosemary and Sun-Dried Tomato Focaccia.* Focaccia is an Italian flat bread similar to pizza but with a taste sensation all its own.

If you want something that's very Southern and very delicious, try *Louisiana Breakfast Puffs* or *Southern Sour Cream Biscuits.* They'll delight everyone in your home, including you.

Here is a favorite with my family - *Philadelphia Butter Cake.* It's so mouth-watering that we make more than one in order to please everyone. Of course, you'll want to try the pizzas, especially the *Mexican Pizza with Cornmeal Crust.* It will truly become a favorite at your home as it is at mine.

CUBAN BREAD

Cooking time: 30 minutes

3 cups all-purpose flour
1 tablespoon sugar
1 teaspoon salt
1 package active dry yeast
1 cup warm water (105°F to 115°F)

- Grease a 9-inch square metal baking pan.

- In a large bowl combine flour, sugar and salt. In a small bowl sprinkle yeast over warm water, stir to dissolve (a small wire whisk works well).

- Pour yeast mixture into flour mixture. Mix well with hands to form a fairly stiff dough. Add more flour if dough is sticky or more water if dough is too dry. Turn out dough onto a floured surface. Knead 2 minutes or until smooth.

- Place dough into an oiled bowl and turn over to oil all sides. Cover with plastic wrap or damp towel. Allow to rise in a warm place for 1 to 1½ hours until double in size.

- Punch down dough and turn onto floured surface. Divide dough into 2 equal pieces. Roll each into an 8-inch rectangle. Starting at a long side, roll each piece of dough "jelly roll fashion" to form a long loaf. Place the loaves side by side in the pan and allow to rise for 30 minutes in a warm place .

- Place wire rack into bowl of oven. Preheat oven to 500°F.

- Reduce oven heat to 400°F and bake bread for 30 minutes. Remove from pan immediately and cool on wire rack.

✔ *Check your owner's manual for preheating time which may vary by manufacturer.*

Wonderful White Bread

Makes 6 Little Loaves

Cooking time: 20 minutes

5½ to 6 cups all-purpose flour

1½ teaspoons salt

1 package active dry yeast

2 cups warm water
(105°F to 115°F)

½ cup vegetable oil

¼ cup honey

1 egg, beaten with 1 tablespoon water

Sesame seeds or poppy seeds (optional)

■ Grease six small 5¼-inchx3¼-inch loaf pans.

■ In a large mixing bowl combine the flour and salt. In a small bowl sprinkle yeast over warm water. Mix with a small wire whisk or fork to dissolve. Add the oil and honey. Stir again.

■ Pour the yeast mixture into the flour mixture. Using your hands, mix until well combined. Add more flour if dough is too sticky or more water if dough is too dry. Turn out dough onto a floured surface and knead for 2 minutes.

■ Place dough into an oiled bowl and turn over to oil all sides. Cover with plastic wrap or damp towel. Allow to rise for 1 to 1½ hours in a warm place until double in size.

■ Punch down dough and turn onto floured surface. Divide dough into 6 equal pieces and shape each into a loaf. Place each loaf into a pan. Brush with beaten egg and sprinkle with seeds if desired. Allow to rise for 30 minutes in a warm place.

■ Place wire rack into bowl of oven. Preheat oven to 500°F.

■ Reduce oven heat to 350°F and bake loaves, three at a time, for 20 minutes. Remove bread from pans immediately and cool on wire racks. Repeat with remaining loaves.

Most recipes in this section call for all-purpose flour. You can use either bleached or unbleached. Both are available at the local supermarket. I prefer unbleached for breads.

CAPE COD CRANBERRY
WHOLE WHEAT MUFFINS

Makes 12

Cooking time: 10 to 12 minutes

¾ cup whole wheat flour

¾ cup all-purpose flour

½ cup old fashioned oatmeal

1 tablespoon baking powder

½ teaspoon salt

1 teaspoon cinnamon

¼ teaspoon ground cloves

1 cup chopped fresh or frozen cranberries, thawed

⅔ cup brown sugar

¾ cup milk

1 egg, lightly beaten

¼ cup vegetable oil

- Grease two 6-cup muffin pans or use paper liners.

- Place wire rack into bowl of oven. Preheat oven to 500°F.

- In a medium bowl combine whole wheat flour, white flour, oatmeal, baking powder, salt, cinnamon, cloves, cranberries and brown sugar. Set aside. Mix together the milk, egg and oil. Pour liquid mixture into dry ingredients and mix until just blended. Do not overmix. Pour batter evenly into muffin cups.

- Reduce oven heat to 425°F. Bake, one pan at a time, for 10 to 12 minutes or until lightly browned. Turn out onto a wire rack to cool.

Easy Pecan Pumpkin Muffins

Makes 12

Cooking time: 8 to 10 minutes

1½ cups buttermilk baking mix (such as Bisquick)
¾ cup brown sugar
2 tablespoons vegetable oil
2 eggs
8-ounces canned pumpkin
2 tablespoons orange juice
1 teaspoon cinnamon
½ teaspoon ginger
¼ teaspoon cloves
¼ teaspoon nutmeg
Grated rind of one orange
½ cup chopped pecans (or walnuts)

- Grease two 6-cup muffin pans or use paper liners.
- Place wire rack into bowl of oven. Preheat oven to 500°F.
- In a medium bowl combine baking mix and brown sugar. Add oil, eggs, pumpkin, orange juice, spices and rind. Mix until well combined. Stir in nuts. Fill muffin cups evenly.
- Reduce oven heat to 425°F. Bake muffins, one pan at a time, for 8 to 10 minutes or until lightly browned. Turn out onto wire rack to cool.

WHILE SOME PEOPLE BELIEVE PUMPKINS ARE AN AMERICAN FRUIT HARVESTED IN THE FALL, THEY ARE SURPRISED TO DISCOVER THAT PUMPKINS ARE ALSO WIDELY HARVESTED IN THE TROPICS. PUMPKINS ARE NOT ONLY GREAT IN PIES, THEY ADD DISTINCTIVE TASTE IN BREADS, CAKES AND MUFFINS.

MID-WEST HARVEST BREAD

Makes 2 Loaves

Cooking time: 30 to 35 minutes

½ cup oatmeal
1 cup boiling water
1 package active dry yeast
3 tablespoons vegetable oil
2 tablespoons molasses
¼ cup barley, cooked and cooled (about 1 cup cooked)
½ cup whole wheat flour
½ cup rye flour
1½ cups all-purpose flour
¼ cup wheat germ
1 teaspoon salt

- Grease two 7½x3½-inch bread pans.

- Place the oatmeal in a large mixing bowl and pour boiling water over oatmeal. Allow to sit 10 minutes or until cooled to 115°F (lukewarm).

- Sprinkle yeast over oatmeal mixture. Stir until well combined and yeast is dissolved. Stir in oil and molasses. Add remaining ingredients.

- With hands, mix to combine all ingredients well. Add more flour if dough is sticky or more water if dough is too dry. Turn out onto a floured surface. Knead until smooth, about 3 to 5 minutes. Place in an oiled bowl and turn dough over to oil all sides. Cover with plastic wrap or damp towel. Allow to rise 1 to 1½ hours in a warm place until double in size.

- Punch down dough. Turn onto floured work surface. Divide dough into two equal pieces and shape into loaves. Place each loaf into a pan. Allow to rise in a warm place for 30 minutes.

- Place wire rack into bowl of oven. Preheat oven to 500°F.

- Reduce oven heat to 350°F. Bake loaves 30 to 35 minutes. Remove from pans immediately and cool on wire rack.

ROSEMARY AND SUN-DRIED TOMATO FOCACCIA

Makes 4

Cooking time: 15 minutes

3 cups all-purpose flour

2 tablespoons chopped fresh rosemary or
2 teaspoons crushed dried rosemary

1 teaspoon salt

1 package active dry yeast

1 cup warm water (105°F to 115°F)

2 tablespoons olive oil

½ cup oil-packed sun-dried tomatoes, drained and chopped

4 teaspoons olive oil

■ Grease four 8 or 9-inch metal baking pans.

■ In a medium bowl combine flour, rosemary and salt. In a separate container sprinkle yeast over the warm water and mix with fork or small whisk to combine. Add olive oil and sun-dried tomatoes. Pour this liquid into the flour mixture. Mix with hands to incorporate the flour and create a moderately stiff dough.

■ Turn dough out onto a floured surface and knead 3 to 5 minutes. Place into an oiled bowl and turn over to oil all sides. Cover and allow to rise 1 hour in a warm place.

■ Punch down dough and turn out onto floured surface. Divide dough into 4 pieces. Roll each piece into a smooth ball. Flatten each ball and roll to form a 7 or 8-inch disk. Poke dough all over with finger to give it a dimpled appearance. Place each disk in a pan. Drizzle 1 teaspoon olive oil on each disk. Allow to rest while oven preheats.

■ Place wire rack into bowl of oven. Preheat oven to 500°F.

■ Reduce oven heat to 400°F. Bake focaccia, one at a time, for 15 minutes or until nicely browned and crisp. Remove from pan immediately. Cool slightly on wire rack. Serve hot, warm or at room temperature.

TUSCAN BLACK PEPPER BREAD

Makes 2 Small Loaves

Cooking time: 30 minutes
Yeast Preparation: 6 hours or overnight

1 cup warm water (105°F to 115°F)
½ package active dry yeast
3 cups all-purpose flour
¼ cup coarsely ground black pepper
1 teaspoon salt

■ Place warm water in a large mixing bowl. Sprinkle yeast over water and stir to combine. Add one cup flour. Mix well with a wooden spoon. Set mixture in a warm place for six hours or overnight. Mixture will become light and full of bubbles.

■ Grease a 9-inch metal baking pan.

■ Mix ground pepper, salt and remaining flour. Add to the yeast and flour mixture. Mix to form a stiff dough. Turn dough out onto a floured surface. Knead 2 to 3 minutes. Place dough into an oiled bowl and turn over to oil all sides. Allow to rise 1½ hours in a warm place until double in size.

■ Punch down dough. Turn out onto a floured surface. Divide into 2 pieces. Shape each piece into a football shaped loaf. Place the loaves side by side in the baking pan. Allow to rise 30 minutes in a warm place.

■ Place wire rack into bowl of oven. Preheat oven to 500°F.

■ Reduce oven heat to 400°F and bake loaves for 30 minutes. Remove from pan immediately and cool on wire rack.

DARK BEER RAISIN PUMPERNICKEL

Makes 2 Loaves

Cooking time: 35 minutes

1 cup all-purpose flour

1 cup rye flour

1 cup whole wheat flour

1½ teaspoons instant coffee granules

1½ teaspoons cocoa powder

¾ cup raisins

1 package active dry yeast

12-ounces dark beer, heated to 105°F to 115°F

1 teaspoon salt

1 tablespoon oil

2 tablespoons molasses

1 egg white, beaten with 1 tablespoon water

■ Grease two 9-inch metal baking pans.

■ In a large mixing bowl combine the all-purpose flour, rye flour, whole wheat flour, coffee, cocoa and raisins. In a separate container sprinkle yeast over warm beer. Stir with a fork or small whisk to combine. Add salt, oil and molasses. Add beer mixture to flour mixture. Mix with hands to incorporate enough flour to make a stiff dough.

■ Turn out onto a floured board and knead 3 to 5 minutes. Place dough into an oiled bowl and turn once to oil surface. Cover with plastic wrap or damp towel. Allow to rise 1 to 1½ hours in a warm place until double in size.

■ Punch down dough. Turn out onto a floured board. Shape into 2 loaves. Place loaves in pans. Allow to rise 30 minutes in a warm place. Gently brush with beaten egg white.

■ Place wire rack into bowl of oven. Preheat oven to 500°F.

■ Reduce oven heat to 400°F. Bake loaves, one at a time, for 35 minutes. Remove bread from pans immediately. Cool on wire rack.

FRENCH PEASANT BREAD

Cooking time: 25 to 30 minutes

1 package active dry yeast
1 cup warm water
(105°F to 115°F)
3 cups all-purpose flour

½ cup wheat germ
1 teaspoon salt
1 teaspoon sugar

■ Grease three 8 or 9-inch baking pans.

■ Sprinkle yeast over warm water in a small bowl. Stir with fork or small whisk to combine. In a large bowl combine the flour, wheat germ, salt and sugar. Pour the yeast mixture into the flour mixture. Mix with hands to incorporate all the flour and make a fairly stiff dough. Add more flour if dough is sticky or more water if dough is too dry.

■ Turn dough out onto a floured surface and knead for 3 to 5 minutes or until smooth. Place dough into an oiled bowl and turn over to oil all sides. Cover with plastic wrap or damp towel and allow to rise 1 hour in a warm place until double in size.

■ Punch down dough. Shape into 3 small loaves about 8-inches long. Place each loaf into a pan and allow to rise for 30 minutes in a warm place.

■ Place wire rack into bowl of oven. Preheat oven to 500°F.

■ Reduce oven heat to 400°F. Bake bread, one loaf at a time, for 15 minutes. Brush with cold water and continue baking for another 15 minutes. Remove from pans immediately and cool on a wire rack.

SOUTHERN SOUR CREAM BISCUITS

Cooking time: 10 minutes

2 cups all-purpose flour
1½ teaspoons sugar
1 tablespoon baking powder
¼ teaspoon baking soda
1 teaspoon salt

6 tablespoons frozen butter or margarine (¾ of a stick)
¼ cup milk
½ cup sour cream

■ Grease two 9-inch metal baking pans.

■ Place wire rack into bowl of oven. Preheat oven to 500°F.

- In a bowl or food processor, combine flour, sugar, baking powder, baking soda and salt. Cut butter or margarine into small bits and sprinkle over top of flour mixture. With pastry blender or pulses of processor blade, work into flour until mixture appears crumbly. With hands or processor, mix in milk and sour cream just until dough holds together.

- Turn dough out onto floured board. Knead 8 to 10 times or just until smooth. Roll out to ½-inch thickness. Cut out 10 to 12 biscuits using a 3-inch biscuit cutter or rim of glass. Dip cutter in flour each time to prevent sticking. Place 5 to 6 biscuits in each pan.

- Reduce oven heat to 375°F. Bake biscuits, one pan at a time, for 10 minutes or until lightly browned.

OLIVE BISCUITS

Makes 8

Cooking time: 10 minutes

2 cups all-purpose flour
3 teaspoons baking powder
1 teaspoon salt
⅓ cup butter or margarine
½ cup pimiento stuffed olives, chopped
¾ cup milk

- Grease a 9-inch baking pan.

- Place wire rack into bowl of oven. Preheat oven to 500°F.

- In a medium bowl combine flour, baking powder and salt. Cut butter or margarine into flour mixture with pastry blender until mixture resembles coarse meal. Mix in olives. Add milk. Combine quickly to incorporate all the flour and make a soft dough.

- Turn out dough onto floured work surface. Knead 8 to 10 times. Pat out to a ¾-inch thickness. Cut with a 2½-inch biscuit cutter. Place in pan.

- Reduce oven heat to 400°F. Bake for 10 minutes or until golden. Serve hot with butter or cream cheese.

Blueberry Muffins with Nutmeg

Makes 12

Cooking time: 10 minutes

1½ cups all-purpose flour	1¼ cups milk
½ cup sugar	1 egg
2 teaspoons baking powder	1 teaspoon vanilla
½ teaspoon salt	⅓ cup vegetable oil
¼ teaspoon nutmeg	1 cup blueberries

- Grease two 6-cup muffin pans or use paper liners.

- Place wire rack into bowl of oven. Preheat oven to 500°F.

- In a large bowl combine flour, sugar, baking powder, salt and nutmeg. In a separate bowl combine the milk, egg, vanilla and oil. Beat well. Pour milk mixture into flour mixture. Mix gently just until combined. Fold in blueberries gently. Spoon batter evenly into muffin cups.

- Reduce oven heat to 350°F. Bake, one pan at a time, for 10 minutes or until lightly browned. Remove from pans immediately.

Dark Onion Rye

Makes 2 Small Loaves

Cooking time: 35 minutes

2 cups all-purpose flour	1 package active dry yeast
1 cup rye flour	1 cup warm water
1 tablespoon caraway seeds	(105°F to 115°F)
1 teaspoon salt	1 tablespoon molasses
2 tablespoons dried onion	2 tablespoons vegetable oil

- Grease two 9-inch metal baking pans.

- Combine white flour, rye flour, caraway seeds, salt and onion in a large bowl. Sprinkle yeast over warm water in a small bowl. Stir with a fork or small whisk to dissolve. Add molasses and oil. Pour yeast mixture into flour mixture. Mix with hands to incorporate flour and make a stiff dough.

- Turn dough out onto a floured surface and knead 3 to 5 minutes. Place dough into an oiled bowl and turn once to oil surface. Cover with plastic wrap or damp towel. Allow to rise 1 to 1½ hours in a warm place until double in size.

- Punch down dough. Turn onto a floured surface. Shape into 2 loaves, round or oval. Place loaves in pans and allow to rise 30 minutes in a warm place.

- Place wire rack into bowl of oven. Preheat oven to 500°F.

- Reduce oven heat to 400°F. Bake loaves, one at a time, for 35 minutes. Remove from pans immediately. Cool on wire rack.

OLD-FASHIONED POPOVERS

Makes 12

Cooking time: 10 to 15 minutes

2 eggs
1 cup all-purpose flour
½ teaspoon salt
1 cup milk
2 tablespoons melted butter

- Grease two 6-cup muffin pans.

- Place wire rack into bowl of oven. Preheat oven to 500°F.

- In a large bowl lightly beat the eggs. Beat in the flour and salt. Stir in the milk. Combine to make a smooth batter. Do not overmix. Add the melted butter and stir.

- Pour the mixture into muffin cups.

- Reduce oven heat to 450°F. Bake popovers for 10 minutes or until very firm. Remove from pans immediately.

OLD-FASHIONED POPOVERS WILL GIVE ANY MEAL EXTRA APPEAL. MY KIDS LOVE THEM. AS A MATTER OF FACT, WHENEVER WE MAKE POPOVERS, MY KIDS THINK WE'RE HAVING GUESTS FOR DINNER. SURPRISE THE FAMILY TONIGHT BY MAKING THESE QUICK AND EASY TREATS.

BANANA BREAD

Cooking time: 45 minutes

1½ cups all-purpose flour
1 teaspoon baking soda
½ teaspoon salt
½ cup brown sugar
¼ cup vegetable oil
2 eggs
½ cup nonfat plain yogurt
1 teaspoon vanilla
1 cup mashed bananas

- Grease a 9x5x3-inch metal baking pan.
- Place wire rack into bowl of oven. Preheat oven to 500°F.
- Combine the flour, baking soda, salt and brown sugar in a large bowl. Add the oil, eggs, yogurt, vanilla and bananas. Beat with an electric mixer just until combined. Pour batter into the greased pan.
- Reduce oven heat to 350°F. Bake 45 minutes. Cool in pan several minutes, then remove from pan and cool on wire rack.

SOFT PRETZELS

Makes 10

Cooking time: 12 minutes

2½ cups all-purpose flour
1 teaspoon salt
½ package active dry yeast
1 cup warm water (105°F to 115°F)
4 teaspoons baking soda
4 cups water
Coarse salt

- Grease two 9-inch metal baking pans.
- Combine flour and salt in a large bowl. Sprinkle yeast over warm water in a separate container. Stir with a fork or small whisk to combine. Pour yeast mixture into flour mixture. Mix with hands to incorporate enough flour to make a stiff dough.

- Turn dough out onto a floured surface. Knead 3 minutes or until smooth. Place dough into an oiled bowl and turn once to oil surface. Cover with plastic wrap or damp towel. Allow to rise about 45 minutes in a warm place.

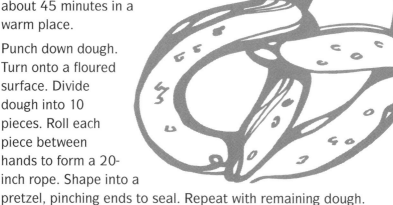

- Punch down dough. Turn onto a floured surface. Divide dough into 10 pieces. Roll each piece between hands to form a 20-inch rope. Shape into a pretzel, pinching ends to seal. Repeat with remaining dough.

- Place wire rack into bowl of oven. Preheat oven to 500°F.

- In a large frying pan dissolve the baking soda in the four cups water and bring water to a boil. Drop the pretzels in one at a time and let them boil 1 minute or until they float. Remove with a slotted spoon and drain.

- Reduce oven heat to 475°F. Place 2 pretzels in a pan, sprinkle with coarse salt and bake for 12 minutes. Repeat this process until all pretzels are baked. Cool on a wire rack. Serve warm with mustard.

FEATHER LIGHT DINNER ROLLS

Makes 24

Cooking time: 12 to 15 minutes

1¼ cups milk
½ cup butter or margarine
1 package active dry yeast
1 egg, lightly beaten
1 teaspoon vanilla
3½ cups all-purpose flour
⅓ cup sugar
1 teaspoon salt
1 egg beaten with 1 tablespoon water
Sesame seeds or poppy seeds (optional)

- Grease three 9-inch metal baking pans.

- In a small saucepan or in microwave, heat milk until just boiling. Add butter or margarine and allow to sit 10 minutes until melted and milk is about 115°F. Sprinkle yeast over milk mixture. Stir with fork or small whisk to combine. Add the egg and vanilla.

- In a large bowl combine the flour, sugar and salt. Pour the liquid ingredients into flour mixture. Mix with hands to make a soft dough.

- Turn dough out onto a floured surface and knead 3 to 5 minutes. Place dough into an oiled bowl and turn once to oil surface. Cover with plastic wrap or damp towel. Allow to rise about 1 to 1½ hours in warm place until double in size.

- Punch down dough. Divide into 24 rolls. Place 8 rolls into each pan. Brush with beaten egg and water mixture and sprinkle with seeds, if desired. Allow to rise 30 minutes in a warm place.

- Place wire rack into bowl of oven. Preheat oven to 500°F.

- Reduce oven heat to 325°F. Bake rolls, one pan at a time, for 12 to 15 minutes or until lightly browned. Turn rolls out onto wire rack to cool.

GRANNY'S SPOONBREAD

Makes 4 Servings

Cooking time: 35 to 40 minutes

½ cup cornmeal (white or yellow)
2 teaspoons sugar
1 teaspoon salt
1½ cups milk
1 tablespoon butter or margarine
1 teaspoon baking powder
2 eggs, separated, whites beaten stiff

■ Grease a 1 quart metal baking pan.

■ Place wire rack into bowl of oven. Preheat oven to 500°F.

■ Combine the cornmeal, sugar and salt in a medium saucepan. Stir in 1 cup of the milk. Cook, stirring constantly, until mixture is very thick and pulls away from the sides of the pan. Remove from heat. Stir in remaining milk, the butter or margarine and baking powder. Beat in the egg yolks. Let cool slightly. Gently fold in beaten egg whites. Pour mixture into pan.

■ Reduce oven heat to 350°F. Bake spoonbread 35 to 40 minutes or until golden and puffed. Serve hot with butter.

GRANNY'S SPOONBREAD USES CORNMEAL IN THE RECIPE. CORNMEAL IS SIMPLY THE GROUND CORN KERNEL. IT IS POPULAR IN BAKING AND USED BY HOME COOKS AND CULINARY PROFESSIONALS ALIKE.

Louisiana Breakfast Puffs

Cooking time: 12 minutes

3 cups all-purpose flour

¾ cup sugar

2 tablespoons baking powder

1 teaspoon salt

½ teaspoon cinnamon

1 cup milk

½ cup vegetable oil

2 eggs, lightly beaten

1 teaspoon vanilla

Topping:

1 cup butter or margarine, melted

1 cup sugar

1 tablespoon cinnamon

- Grease two 6-cup muffin pans or use paper liners.

- Place wire rack into bowl of oven. Preheat oven to 500°F.

- Combine flour, sugar, baking powder, salt and cinnamon in a large bowl. Combine milk, oil, eggs and vanilla in a separate bowl. Pour milk mixture into flour mixture. Stir until just combined. Spoon batter evenly into muffin cups.

- Reduce oven heat to 350°F. Bake, one pan at a time, for 12 minutes. Cool for a minute before turning them out onto a wire rack.

- Melt butter or margarine and transfer to a bowl. In another bowl, combine sugar and cinnamon. Quickly coat each muffin in butter or margarine and let excess drip off. Roll each in cinnamon sugar.

CHEESY COFFEE BUNS

Makes 8

Cooking time: 15 to 20 minutes

1 package active dry yeast

1 cup warm water
(105°F to 115°F)

2½ cups all-purpose flour

⅓ cup sugar

Pinch salt

1 egg yolk

¼ cup sour cream

½ cup butter or margarine

Filling:

6-ounces cream cheese, softened

1 egg

⅓ cup sugar

½ teaspoon vanilla

Glaze:

½ cup apricot or peach jam

■ Grease eight individual 3-inch foil muffin cups.*

■ In a small bowl sprinkle yeast over warm water. Stir with fork or whisk to dissolve.

■ In a large bowl combine flour, sugar and salt. Add egg yolk, sour cream, butter or margarine and yeast mixture. Mix with hands to form a soft dough.

■ Turn out dough onto a floured work surface. Knead 3 minutes. Place dough into an oiled bowl and turn once to oil surface. Cover with plastic wrap or damp towel and allow to rise 1½ hours in a warm place until double in size.

■ Prepare filling: In a small bowl combine cream cheese, egg, sugar and vanilla. Beat with electric mixer until smooth.

■ Punch down dough. Divide into 8 pieces. Roll each piece into a 7-inch circle. Line each muffin tin with a circle of dough. Put about 2 tablespoons of filling in each cup. Bring edges of dough together and pinch to seal. Allow to rise 30 minutes in a warm place.

■ Place wire rack into bowl of oven. Preheat oven to 500°F.

■ Reduce oven heat to 350°F. Bake buns 15 to 20 minutes or until lightly browned. Turn out onto wire rack to cool.

■ Heat jam in a small saucepan. Force jam through a strainer or whirl in blender until smooth. Brush cooled buns with glaze.

* You can also use a muffin pan with 3-inch cups. Grease cups or use foil cups. Put ½-inch water in cups not filled with dough.

EASY RASPBERRY COFFEE CAKE

Makes 8 Servings

Cooking time: 45 minutes

1½ cups all-purpose flour
½ cup sugar
1 teaspoon baking powder
½ teaspoon baking soda
Pinch salt
6 tablespoons butter or margarine
1 egg, beaten
½ cup sour cream, regular or low-fat
1 teaspoon vanilla
1 cup raspberry preserves

- Grease an 8x8-inch metal baking pan.

- Place wire rack into bowl of oven. Preheat oven to 500°F.

- In a medium bowl combine flour, sugar, baking powder, baking soda and salt. Using a pastry blender, cut in butter or margarine until mixture resembles fine crumbs. Mix in the egg, sour cream and vanilla.

- Spread half the batter in the bottom of the pan. Spread preserves over batter. Drop remaining batter by large spoonfuls over raspberry preserves.

- Reduce oven heat to 350°F. Bake cake for 45 minutes or until golden. Cool in pan on wire rack. Sprinkle with powdered sugar if desired.

ORANGE RAISIN SCONES

Makes 8

Cooking time: 25 minutes

2 cups all-purpose flour
⅓ cup sugar
1½ teaspoons baking powder
½ teaspoon baking soda
½ teaspoon salt
6 tablespoons butter or margarine
½ cup raisins
1 teaspoon finely shredded orange rind
½ cup fresh orange juice
¼ cup plain yogurt or buttermilk

■ Grease a 9-inch round cake pan.

■ In a large bowl combine flour, sugar, baking powder, baking soda and salt. Cut in butter or margarine using a pastry blender. Add raisins and rind. Mix in lightly. Add orange juice and yogurt or buttermilk. Mix lightly with hands to form a dough. Dough will be very moist.

■ With floured hands, pat dough into cake pan. With a sharp knife, cut dough into 8 pie shaped wedges.

■ Place wire rack into bowl of oven. Preheat oven to 500°F.

■ Reduce oven heat to 350°F. Bake scones for 25 minutes. When done, cool slightly and recut wedges.

FELICITY SIMPSON'S CURRANT SCONES

Makes 24

Cooking time: 10 to 15 minutes

2 cups all-purpose flour
1 teaspoon baking powder
¼ teaspoon baking soda
Pinch salt
½ cup (1 stick) cold butter
½ cup currants
½ cup evaporated milk
1 tablespoon water

■ Place wire rack into bowl of oven. Preheat oven to 500°F.

■ In a medium sized bowl or food processor bowl combine flour, baking powder, baking soda and salt. Cut butter into small pieces, about 20 and scatter on top of flour mixture. Using a pastry blender or processor, work butter into flour until mixture appears crumbly and the particles are the size of peas. If using processor, transfer mixture to a bowl.

■ With hands, mix in currants, evaporated milk and water. Mix gently to form a sticky dough. Turn out onto a floured board. Knead gently 10 times. Roll out dough to ½-inch thickness. Cut dough into 3-inch circles using a cookie cutter or the rim of a glass. Cut each circle in half. Place 12 halves into each of two ungreased 9-inch metal baking pans.

■ Reduce oven heat to 375°F. Bake, one pan at a time, for 10 to 15 minutes or until golden.

CURRANTS RESEMBLE RAISINS. THEY ARE THE DRIED FRUIT OF SEVERAL SPECIES OF BERRIES THAT ARE THE SIZE OF THE SMALL GRAPES OF THE MEDITERRANEAN REGION. IN ALL, CURRANTS CAN BE FOUND IN THREE COLORS: RED, WHITE AND BLACK.

SOUR CREAM COFFEE CAKE

Makes 8 Servings

Cooking time: 30 to 35 minutes

Topping:
2 tablespoons brown sugar
1 tablespoon all-purpose flour
1 teaspoon cinnamon
1 tablespoon butter, softened
½ cup chopped pecans

½ cup butter or margarine
¾ cup packed brown sugar
1 teaspoon vanilla
1 egg, lightly beaten
½ cup sour cream
1 ¼ cups all-purpose flour
Pinch salt
1 teaspoon baking powder
¼ teaspoon baking soda

- Grease an 8x8-inch square metal baking pan.

- Place wire rack into bowl of oven. Preheat oven to 500°F.

- Combine all topping ingredients except nuts. Mix with fingers until crumbly. Add nuts.

- In a mixer bowl cream butter or margarine and sugar until light and fluffy. Beat in vanilla, egg and sour cream. In a separate container combine flour, salt, baking powder and baking soda. Add flour mixture in thirds to sour cream and egg mixture, beating well after each addition. Pour half the batter into the pan and sprinkle with half the topping. Pour in remaining batter and top with remaining topping.

- Reduce oven heat to 350°F. Bake cake 30 to 35 minutes or until golden. Allow cake to cool 10 minutes before removing from pan.

BRAIDED BAGEL BREAD

Makes 2 Loaves

Cooking time: 20 to 25 minutes

1 package active dry yeast
3½ cups all-purpose flour
1 cup warm water (105°F to 115°F)
2 tablespoons sugar
1½ teaspoons salt

- Grease two 7½x3½-inch bread pans.

- In a large mixer bowl combine yeast and 1 cup of flour. In a separate container combine water, sugar and salt. Add to yeast mixture. Beat at low speed with electric mixer for 30 seconds to incorporate flour. Beat 5 minutes on high speed. By hand, stir in remaining flour to make a stiff dough that is not sticky.

- Turn dough out onto a floured surface and knead until smooth, about 3 to 5 minutes. Cover dough with plastic wrap or damp towel and allow to rest 15 minutes.

- Divide dough in half. Cut each half into 3 pieces. Shape the 3 pieces into ropes about 8-inches long. Braid 3 ropes together to form loaves. Place loaves in pan and allow to rise 20 minutes in a warm place.

- Place wire rack into bowl of oven. Preheat oven to 500°F.

- Reduce oven heat to 350°F. Gently brush top of loaves with small amount of water. Bake loaves for 15 minutes, brush with water and bake for another 5 to 10 minutes. Remove from pans immediately and cool on a wire rack.

PHILADELPHIA BUTTER CAKE

Makes 2 Cakes

Cooking time: 25 minutes

1½ teaspoons active dry yeast
¼ cup warm water
(105° to 115°F)
2¼ cups all-purpose flour
⅓ cup sugar
½ teaspoon salt
1 cup milk, heated to 115°F
¼ cup butter
1 egg
1 teaspoon vanilla

Topping:
¾ cup sugar
1 stick butter, at room temperature
¼ teaspoon salt
1 egg
¾ cup flour
2 tablespoons water
2 tablespoons dark corn syrup
1½ teaspoons vanilla extract

- Grease two 8 or 9-inch cake pans.

- In a small container, sprinkle yeast over warm water. Set aside.

- In a large mixing bowl combine flour, sugar and salt. In a small bowl combine the warm milk and butter. Stir to melt butter. Beat in the egg. Add vanilla and yeast mixture.

- Pour the liquid ingredients into the flour mixture. Mix with hands to form a soft dough. Turn out dough onto a floured surface. Knead 1 minute, adding more flour if necessary. Place the dough into an oiled bowl and turn once to oil surface. Allow to rise 1 to 1½ hours in a warm place until double in size.

- Punch down dough. Divide dough into 2 pieces. Roll each piece into a rough circle. Place each piece into a pan. Poke dough all over with finger to form "dimples." Spread dough to come half way up the sides of the pan.

- Make Topping: Place ingredients in a small mixer bowl, beat at high speed for about 2 minutes or until fluffy. Pour half of topping on each pan of dough. Smooth with a spatula. Let cakes rise 20 minutes in a warm place.

- Place wire rack into bowl of oven. Preheat oven to 500°F.

- Reduce oven heat to 375°F. Bake cakes, one at a time, for 25 minutes or until puffed and golden.

FRENCH CURRANT BUNS

Makes 24

Cooking time: 15 to 20 minutes

4 cups all-purpose flour
⅓ cup sugar
½ teaspoon salt
½ teaspoon cinnamon
¼ teaspoon nutmeg
¾ cup currants
1¾ cups milk
¼ cup butter or margarine
1 package of active dry yeast

■ Grease three 9-inch baking pans.

■ Combine the flour, sugar, salt, cinnamon, nutmeg and currants in a large bowl. Heat milk to just boiling. Remove from heat and add butter or margarine. Allow to sit until butter is completely melted and milk is cooled to 115°F, about 10 minutes. Sprinkle yeast over milk mixture. Stir to combine.

■ Pour yeast mixture into flour mixture. Mix with hands to incorporate enough flour to make a stiff dough. Turn dough out onto floured surface. Knead 3 minutes. Place dough into an oiled bowl and turn once to oil surface. Cover with plastic wrap or damp towel. Allow to rise 1 hour in a warm place until double in size.

■ Punch down dough. Turn out onto floured surface. Pull off 24 golf ball sized pieces of dough. Shape into smooth balls. Place 8 balls in each pan. Allow to rise 30 minutes in a warm place.

■ Place wire rack into bowl of oven. Preheat oven to 500°F.

■ Reduce oven heat to 400°F. Bake buns, one pan at a time, for 15 to 20 minutes. Remove from pans immediately. Cool on wire racks.

OATMEAL RAISIN WALNUT BREAD

Makes 2 Loaves

Cooking time: 30 minutes

¾ cup old fashioned oatmeal

1 teaspoon salt

1 cup boiling water

½ cup nonfat plain yogurt

2 tablespoons vegetable oil

2 tablespoons brown sugar

1 package active dry yeast

¼ cup warm water
(105°F to 115°F)

½ cup raisins

½ cup walnuts

3 cups all-purpose flour

Filling:

2 tablespoons butter or margarine

⅔ cup brown sugar

2 teaspoons cinnamon

- ■ Grease two 7½x3½-inch bread pans.

- ■ In a large mixing bowl combine oatmeal, salt and boiling water. Allow oatmeal to soften 1 minute. Stir in yogurt, oil and brown sugar. In a separate container, sprinkle yeast over warm water and mix with fork. Add yeast mixture to oatmeal mixture. Stir in raisins and nuts. Add flour. Mix to form a dough that is not too sticky.

- ■ Turn out dough onto a floured surface. Knead for 3 minutes. Place dough into an oiled bowl and turn once to oil surface. Let rise 1 to 1½ hours in a warm place until double in size.

- ■ Punch down dough. Turn out onto floured surface. Divide into 2 pieces. Roll each piece into a rectangle about ¼-inch thick. Spread each with 1 tablespoon of butter and sprinkle with ⅓ cup sugar and 1 teaspoon cinnamon. Bring the short ends of the dough to the center, then roll the dough, jelly roll fashion. Place each in a pan. Allow to rise 30 minutes in a warm place.

- ■ Place wire rack into bowl of oven. Preheat oven to 500°F.

- ■ Reduce oven heat to 375°. Bake the loaves for 30 minutes. Turn out of pans immediately onto wire rack to cool.

SPICY SWEET POTATO MUFFINS

Makes 12

Cooking time: 45 to 50 minutes

1 large or 2 small sweet potatoes, washed
1½ cups all-purpose flour
¾ cup packed brown sugar
½ teaspoon salt
2 teaspoons baking powder
1 teaspoon baking soda
1 teaspoon cinnamon
½ teaspoon ginger
¼ teaspoon cloves
¼ cup vegetable oil
¾ cup milk
1 egg

- Grease two 6-cup muffin pans or use paper liners.
- Place wire rack into bowl of oven. Preheat oven to 500°F.
- Reduce oven heat to 400°F. Bake sweet potatoes 20 to 25 minutes or until tender when pierced with fork. Cool, peel and puree in food processor. One-half cup will be needed for recipe.
- Preheat oven to 500°F again.
- In a large bowl combine flour, sugar, salt, baking powder, baking soda, cinnamon, ginger and cloves. In a separate container combine the oil, milk and egg. Mix well with wire whisk. Blend in sweet potato puree. Pour sweet potato mixture into flour mixture. Mix just until all ingredients are combined. Pour batter evenly into muffin cups.
- Reduce oven heat to 350°F. Bake muffins, one pan at a time, for 25 minutes or until lightly browned. Remove from pans immediately and cool on wire rack.

EASY PIZZA DOUGH

Makes Four 9-inch Pizzas

Cooking time: 20 minutes

*1 package active
dry yeast*

*1⅔ cups warm water
(105°F to 115°F)*

1 tablespoon olive oil

*1 teaspoon sugar
or honey*

*4 to 4¼ cups
all-purpose flour*

½ teaspoon salt

- Grease four 9-inch metal baking pans.

- Place wire rack into bowl of oven. Preheat oven to 500°F.

- In a large bowl, sprinkle yeast over warm water. Add oil and sugar or honey. Mix with a whisk or fork to combine. Add flour and salt to yeast mixture. Mix with hands to form a stiff dough.

- Turn dough out onto a floured surface and knead for 2 minutes. Place dough into an oiled bowl and turn once to oil surface. Cover and allow to rise for 50 minutes to 1 hour in a warm place.

- Punch down dough. Turn out onto a floured surface and divide into four pieces. Roll each piece into a rough circle. Place each piece into a pan. With fingers, spread dough so that it comes approximately ¾-inch up the sides of the pan.

- Reduce oven heat to 400°F and bake dough for 15 minutes until crust is golden brown. Top with desired toppings, such as pizza sauce and shredded cheese and continue baking for 5 minutes until cheese is melted.

Traditional Cheese Pizza Toppings (per pizza):
½ cup crushed tomatoes or tomato sauce
½ cup grated mozzarella cheese
Garlic and herbs to taste

WHOLE WHEAT PIZZA WITH CAPOCOLLO AND TWO CHEESES

Makes Four 9-inch Pizzas

Cooking time: 20 minutes per pizza

1 recipe Easy Pizza Dough (page 69)
Substitute 1 cup whole wheat flour for 1 cup of white flour.

Topping:
16 thin slices provolone cheese
16 thin slices capocollo ham
16 thin slices mozzarella cheese

■ Bake as directed in Easy Pizza Dough recipe (page 69) or until cheese is melted and crust is golden.

PIZZA PRIMAVERA

Makes Four 9-inch Pizzas

Cooking time: 20 minutes per pizza

1 recipe Easy Pizza Dough (page 69)
1 cup frozen chopped broccoli, defrosted
1 cup chopped zucchini, cooked 1 minute in boiling water, drained and patted dry
4 scallions, chopped
1 cup red pepper, seeded and chopped (approximately 1 large pepper)
2 teaspoons garlic, minced
4 fresh plum tomatoes, cut into ¼-inch slices
2 to 3 cups shredded mozzarella or other melting cheese
4 tablespoons fresh basil, chopped or 1 tablespoon dried

■ Combine the broccoli, zucchini, scallions, red pepper and garlic. Shape dough and fill pans. Top each pizza with about 1 cup of the vegetable garlic mixture, the tomato slices and the desired amount of cheese. Sprinkle with basil and bake as directed in Easy Pizza Dough recipe (page 69) or until cheese is melted and pizza crust is golden. Slice and serve hot.

MEXICAN PIZZA WITH CORNMEAL CRUST

Makes Four 9-inch Pizzas

Cooking time: 20 minutes

1 recipe Easy Pizza Dough (page 69)
Substitute ½ cup cornmeal for ½ cup of the flour.

Mexican Topping:
1 cup crushed tomatoes
1 cup prepared salsa
1 teaspoon cumin
2 cups grated Monterey Jack cheese
Jalapeno peppers, sliced, as desired
Black olives, as desired

■ Combine tomatoes, salsa and cumin. Spread ¼ cup of mixture on each baked pizza dough. Top with cheese. If desired, add peppers and olives. Bake as directed in Easy Pizza Dough recipe (page 69) or until cheese is melted and crust is golden.

ALMOST EVERYONE THE WORLD OVER LOVES PIZZA, BUT NOT EVERY PIZZA IS ITALIAN. HERE'S A VARIATION THAT HAS SOUTH-OF-THE-BORDER FLAIR. IT IS PERFECT FOR A FAMILY MEAL OR IT CAN MAKE A WONDERFUL PARTY APPETIZER.

JALAPENO CORN MUFFINS

Cooking time: 12 to 15 minutes

1 cup all-purpose flour

1 cup yellow cornmeal

2 tablespoons sugar

2 teaspoons baking powder

½ teaspoon salt

1 cup milk

1 egg, lightly beaten

¼ cup vegetable oil

½ cup grated Monterey Jack cheese

½ cup pickled jalapeno peppers, sliced

- ■ Grease two 6-cup muffin pans or use paper liners.

- ■ Place wire rack into bowl of oven. Preheat oven to 500°F.

- ■ In a large bowl mix the flour, cornmeal, sugar, baking powder and salt. In a small bowl mix the milk, egg and oil. Pour liquid ingredients into dry ingredients and mix until just blended. Do not overmix. Stir in the cheese and peppers. Pour batter evenly into muffin cups.

- ■ Reduce oven heat to 425°F. Bake, one pan at a time, for 12 to 15 minutes or until lightly browned. Turn out onto a wire rack to cool.

Thai
Spiced
Cornish
Hens, *p.78*

Top:
Rolled Boneless Turkey Breast with Pepperoni and Mozzarella, *p.83*

Bottom:
Tequila Lime Pork Tenderloin with Enchilada Cream Sauce, *p.87*

Top:
Ragin' Cajun Meat Loaf, *p.85*

Cutting Board:
Ham and Pineapple Kabobs with Chutney Curry Glaze, *p.89*

Glass Plate:
Caribbean Chicken Diablo, *p.78*

MEAT & POULTRY

*O*ven *Fried Chicken with Southwest Spices* never tasted as good as it does in a Countertop Convection Oven. And if you like a great meat loaf, then you simply must try **Ragin' Cajun Meat Loaf** for a delectable taste that is right out of Louisiana.

*W*hen company comes, my family loves to serve **Boneless Pork Chops with Orange Dijon Parmesan Crust**. It's a hit that will make you the star of the evening or any time of day you serve it. **Veal Chops Stuffed with Spinach and Three Cheeses** is another attention getter.

*M*y personal favorite is **Rolled Boneless Turkey Breast with Pepperoni and Mozzarella.** My mouth is watering just thinking about it. You'll have a hard time deciding which of these recipes is the best thing you've ever tasted, but you'll sure have fun trying!

THAI SPICED CORNISH HENS

Cooking time: 30 minutes
Marinate: Several hours or overnight

3 tablespoons Thai chili paste (red or green)*

2 tablespoons vegetable oil

2 tablespoons fresh lime juice

2 cornish hens, about 1½ pounds each, backbones removed

* Available at Oriental groceries and some supermarkets

■ Combine chili paste, oil and lime juice in a small bowl. Rub mixture all over hens. Place hens in a plastic bag and seal with twist tie. Refrigerate several hours or overnight.

■ Place wire rack into bowl of oven. Preheat oven to 500°F.

■ Reduce oven heat to 450°F. Remove hens from marinade and place directly on wire rack, breast side down. Bake for 30 minutes or until inner thigh registers 180° on meat thermometer.

CARIBBEAN CHICKEN DIABLO

Cooking time: 35 minutes

½ cup pickled jalapeno peppers

2 tablespoons liquid from peppers

2 tablespoons yellow mustard

1 small onion finely chopped

2 tablespoons orange juice

1 teaspoon dried rosemary, crushed

1 teaspoon dried thyme, crushed

1 teaspoon dried basil, crushed

½ teaspoon coarse black pepper

1 tablespoon Pickapeppa sauce or bottled steak sauce

3½ pound frying chicken, cut into 12 pieces, skin removed

■ Place wire rack into bowl of oven. Preheat oven to 500°F.

■ Combine all the ingredients except the chicken in a food processor. Process 30 seconds. Transfer mixture to a shallow baking dish. Add chicken, turning to coat well.

■ Reduce oven heat to 350°F. Bake chicken for 30 minutes. Raise heat to 500°F and bake 5 more minutes.

Oven Fried Chicken with Southwest Spices

Makes 6 Servings

Cooking time: 12 to 15 minutes

1 tablespoon vegetable oil

½ cup buttermilk baking mix (such as Bisquick)

1 tablespoon chili powder

½ teaspoon cumin

½ teaspoon coriander

1 teaspoon Adobo seasoning or seasoned salt

½ teaspoon coarse black pepper

4 boneless, skinless chicken breast halves

1 egg, beaten

- Place wire rack into bowl of oven. Preheat oven to 500°F.

- Pour vegetable oil in bottom of a 9-inch baking pan. Tilt pan to coat with oil.

- In a large shallow bowl mix well the baking mix, chili powder, cumin, coriander, Adobo or seasoned salt and pepper. Dip each breast half in beaten egg. Coat evenly in baking mix mixture. Place breast in oiled pan. Turn once to coat both sides with a little oil.

- Reduce oven heat to 400°F. Bake chicken 12 to 15 minutes or until cooked through. Serve immediately with salsa if desired.

AT THE SUPERMARKET YOU CAN TELL IF THE CHICKEN PARTS YOU PURCHASE ARE FRESH OR HAVE BEEN FROZEN. LOOK AT THE TRAY THEY ARE IN. IF THERE IS A LOT OF LIQUID IN THE TRAY WITH THE CHICKEN, CHANCES ARE THAT THE CHICKEN HAS BEEN FROZEN.

✔ *Check your owner's manual for preheating time which may vary by manufacturer.*

ROASTED CHICKEN NICOISE

Makes 2 Servings

Cooking time: 25 minutes

2 tablespoons olive oil

1 boneless, skinless chicken breast

¼ pound green beans, trimmed and cut into 1-inch pieces

4 red new potatoes, scrubbed and cut into ¾-inch cubes

2 cups romaine lettuce, torn into bite-sized pieces

2 plum tomatoes, cut into ½-inch cubes

2 teaspoons capers

2 tablespoons Nicoise olives

Dressing:

1 anchovy fillet

½ teaspoon garlic, minced

1 teaspoon Dijon mustard

1 tablespoon red wine vinegar

2 tablespoons olive oil

Salt and pepper

■ Place wire rack into bowl of oven. Preheat oven to 500°F. Coat a 9-inch baking pan with olive oil.

■ Cut chicken breast into 4 equal strips. Place chicken, beans and potatoes in pan. Toss to coat with oil. Sprinkle lightly with salt and pepper. Chicken should rest on top of vegetables.

■ Reduce oven heat to 400°F. Bake 25 minutes, stirring every 5 minutes.

■ Make dressing while chicken cooks. Mash anchovy fillet with a fork. Add garlic, mustard and vinegar. Blend with a whisk. Whisk in oil. Season with salt and pepper.

■ As soon as chicken is done, toss romaine with dressing. Put dressed romaine on serving plates and top with chicken, beans and potatoes. Top each serving with diced tomatoes, capers and olives.

Here's a chart that shows the nutritional value of chicken, based on a cooked 3.5 ounce serving:

	Calories	Total Fat (grams)	Saturated Fat (grams)	Cholesterol (milligrams)
Dark and light meat, roasted, with skin	239	14	4	88
Dark meat, roasted, without skin	205	10	3	93
Light meat , roasted, without skin	173	5	1	85

Source: USDA Agriculture Handbooks

Cornish Hens With Lemon And Herbs

Makes 4 Servings

Cooking time: 20 to 25 minutes
Marinate: 8 hours or overnight

2 Cornish Hens about 1¼ to 1½ pounds each

Marinade:
½ cup fresh lemon juice
¼ cup olive oil
2 teaspoons dried oregano
1 teaspoon dried thyme
1 tablespoon dried rosemary, crumbled
2 teaspoons freshly ground black pepper

- Remove backbones from hens so they lie flat.
- Combine lemon juice, olive oil, oregano, thyme, rosemary and pepper in a 9x13 inch glass baking dish. Add chicken to marinade and turn once to coat. Let marinate in the refrigerator at least 8 hours or overnight.
- Place wire rack into bowl of oven. Preheat oven to 500°F.
- Remove chicken from marinade. Save marinade.
- Reduce oven heat to 475°F. Cook hens 20 to 25 minutes, skin side down. Baste with marinade every 5 minutes. Turn the hens once. Bake until hens are tender and no longer pink.

SAVORY CONFETTI TURKEY LOAF

Makes 4 to 6 Servings

Cooking time: 35 minutes

1 slice white bread

1 egg

2 teaspoons Worcestershire sauce

½ teaspoon salt

½ teaspoon black pepper

1 teaspoon Italian seasoning

¼ cup onion, chopped

1 cup carrot, chopped

⅓ cup green pepper, chopped

1 tablespoon pimiento, chopped

1¼ pounds ground turkey

■ Place wire rack into bowl of oven. Preheat oven to 500°F.

■ Quickly place bread under running water until just soaked. Place in a large bowl with egg, Worcestershire sauce, salt, pepper, Italian seasoning, onion, carrot, green pepper and pimiento. Mix until well blended and bread is completely broken up. Add turkey. Mix until well combined. Shape into a loaf about 9-inches long. Place loaf in a 9-inch loaf pan.

■ Reduce oven heat to 350°F. Bake 35 minutes.

BONELESS TURKEY BREAST WITH PESTO AND BALSAMIC VINEGAR

Makes 4 to 6 Servings

Cooking time: 45 to 50 minutes
Marinate: 1 to 3 hours

2 tablespoons prepared pesto sauce

1 tablespoon balsamic vinegar

1 teaspoon garlic, minced

1   2¼ pound boneless turkey breast, skin attached

■ In a small bowl whisk together pesto, balsamic vinegar and garlic until smooth. Turn back breast skin and spread breast meat with half of the pesto mixture. Replace breast skin and hold in place with toothpicks, if necessary. Turn breast over. Spread meat covered side with remaining pesto mixture. Refrigerate 1 to 3 hours.

■ Place wire rack into bowl of oven. Preheat oven to 500°F.

■ Place turkey in a 9-inch baking pan, skin side down. Reduce oven heat to 350°F. Cook turkey 20 minutes. Turn skin side up and cook another 25 to 30 minutes. Slice thinly to serve.

ROLLED BONELESS TURKEY BREAST WITH PEPPERONI AND MOZZARELLA

Makes 4 to 6 Servings

Cooking time: 45 to 50 minutes
Marinate: 1 to 3 hours

Marinade:

3 tablespoons olive oil

2 tablespoons fresh lemon juice

1 teaspoon garlic

Salt and pepper

1   2¼ pound (approx.) skinless boneless turkey breast

¼ pound thinly sliced pepperoni

¼ pound shredded mozzarella cheese

1 cup water

½ cup dry white wine

½ cup tomato paste

3 tablespoons cold butter or margarine

■ In a large baking dish (do not use aluminum) combine olive oil, lemon juice, garlic, salt and pepper.

■ Lay turkey breast on a flat work surface, skin side down. Place a large sheet of plastic wrap over breast and pound with a wooden mallet to a thickness of about ¾ of an inch. Place turkey in oil/lemon marinade. Turn to coat. Cover and refrigerate 1 to 3 hours.

■ Place wire rack into bowl of oven. Preheat oven to 500°F.

■ Remove turkey from marinade. Place on a flat work surface. Spread the breast with pepperoni, then cheese. Roll up jelly roll fashion and tie with kitchen string to secure. Place in a 9-inch nonstick coated metal baking pan.

■ Reduce oven heat to 350°F. Cook 45 to 50 minutes. Cover with foil if turkey or pan drippings are getting too brown. You may also reduce oven heat to 325°F.

■ Remove string and place turkey on a serving platter. Add water to baking pan and stir to loosen any browned bits from pan. Transfer water to a saucepan on stove top burner. Add wine. Cook over medium heat for 5 minutes. Stir in tomato paste and simmer 2 minutes. Whisk in butter or margarine, 1 tablespoon at a time. Slice turkey into ½-inch slices. Serve with sauce.

PEPPERED BEEF FILLET

Makes 4 Servings

Cooking time: 45 minutes to 1 hour

2 teaspoons black peppercorns
2 teaspoons pink peppercorns
2 teaspoons green peppercorns
1   3-pound beef fillet roast
Salt

- ■ Place wire rack into bowl of oven. Preheat oven to 500°F.

- ■ Crush the peppercorns with a mortar and pestle or electric coffee grinder. Mix the crushed peppercorns and press them into the surface of the roast, coating the meat evenly. Season meat with salt to taste.

- ■ Reduce oven heat to 400°F. Place fillet directly on wire rack. Cook 45 minutes to 1 hour. Cover with foil if the roast is browning too quickly. Secure foil with toothpicks or small skewers. Allow roast to rest 10 minutes before slicing.

WINE BRAISED BRISKET

Makes 4 Servings

Cooking time: 2 hours
Marinate: 5 hours or overnight

2 pounds beef brisket
2 cups dry red wine
¼ cup fresh onion or 2 tablespoons dried minced onion
2 teaspoons garlic, chopped
2 tablespoons Dijon mustard
2 tablespoons flour
Water as needed, about 1 cup

- ■ Pierce meat all over with the tip of a small sharp knife. Combine wine and onion in large baking dish (do not use aluminum). Place meat in dish and turn to coat. Spread each side with garlic and mustard. Allow to marinate in refrigerator 5 hours or overnight.

- ■ Place wire rack into bowl of oven. Preheat oven to 500°F.

- Place 2 tablespoons flour in an 8x8-inch baking dish (do not use aluminum). Add marinade and stir to combine. Add meat. Place a piece of foil the same size as the baking dish directly on wire rack. Place dish on foil.

- Reduce oven heat to 475°F. Bake meat uncovered for 20 minutes. Reduce oven heat to 350°F. Cover dish tightly with foil and continue baking for 1 hour and 40 minutes. Check every 20 to 30 minutes, adding water to keep sauce from becoming too thick or dry when necessary. Meat is done when it is tender.

- Remove meat from sauce. Slice thinly and serve with sauce.

RAGIN' CAJUN MEAT LOAF

Makes 4 to 6 Servings

Cooking time: 40 to 50 minutes

1 egg

1 slice white bread, made into crumbs

½ cup tomato juice

1¼ pounds ground beef

1 tablespoon bottled steak sauce

¼ teaspoon dried thyme

¼ teaspoon dried basil

½ teaspoon pepper

½ teaspoon garlic, minced

¾ cup chopped onion

2 tablespoons prepared Cajun seasoning

- Place wire rack into bowl of oven. Preheat oven to 500°F.

- In a large bowl beat egg, bread crumbs and tomato juice. Add ground beef, steak sauce, thyme, basil, pepper, garlic, onion and Cajun seasoning. Mix well with hands. Shape into a loaf, 8½-inches long. Place in a 9-inch loaf pan.

- Reduce oven heat to 350°F. Bake 40 to 50 minutes or until nicely browned.

CAJUN FOOD IS EXTREMELY POPULAR TODAY. WHILE ITS ROOTS ARE PLANTED IN THE DEEP SOUTH, IT HAS GAINED UNIVERSAL APPEAL.

BONELESS PORK CHOPS WITH ORANGE DIJON PARMESAN CRUST

Makes 4 Servings

Cooking time: 20 minutes
Marinate: 1 to 3 hours

8 boneless pork chops, 2-ounces each
3 tablespoons Dijon mustard
2 tablespoons orange marmalade
1 teaspoon garlic, minced
½ cup dry bread crumbs
¼ cup grated Parmesan cheese

- Place wire rack into bowl of oven. Preheat oven to 500°F.

- Trim any excess fat from chops. Mix mustard, marmalade and garlic in a shallow glass dish large enough to hold the chops in a single layer. Add chops. Turn in mixture to coat. Marinate in refrigerator for 1 to 3 hours.

- Combine bread crumbs and cheese on a large flat plate. Roll chops in crumbs to coat.

- Reduce oven heat to 425°F. Place chops directly on wire rack. Bake for 20 minutes or until nicely browned. Serve immediately.

PORK TENDERLOIN ROLLS STUFFED WITH CHEESE AND CHILIES

Makes 4 Servings

Cooking time: 15 minutes

Sauce:
8-ounce jar prepared mild salsa
½ cup crushed tomatoes
⅓ cup chicken broth
1 can mild green chili, chopped

1 pound pork tenderloin, cut crosswise into 8 slices pounded thin between sheets of plastic wrap
½ pound Monterey Jack, cut into 8 pieces
2 pickled whole jalapeno peppers, seeded and cut lengthwise in 8 strips.
2 tablespoons vegetable oil

- Combine salsa, crushed tomatoes, broth and chilies in saucepan. Simmer 10 minutes.

- Place wire rack into bowl of oven. Preheat oven to 500°F.

- Lay flattened tenderloin slices on a flat work surface. In the center of each pork slice, arrange 1 piece of cheese and 1 strip of jalapeno pepper. Fold the ends over the filling and roll the pork up tightly. Secure with a toothpick. Brush rolls with 2 tablespoons of vegetable oil. Arrange rolls in a 9-inch baking pan.

- Reduce oven heat to 450°F. Bake rolls 15 minutes or until browned and cooked through. Serve rolls with reheated sauce.

TEQUILA LIME PORK TENDERLOIN WITH ENCHILADA CREAM SAUCE

Makes 4 Servings

Cooking time: 20 minutes
Marinate: 1 hour

2 1-pound pork tenderloins

Marinade:
1 tablespoon lime juice
2 teaspoons lime rind, grated
2 teaspoons garlic, minced
1 tablespoon vegetable oil
1 teaspoon salt, preferably coarse
1 tablespoon tequila (optional)

Sauce:
1 cup canned enchilada sauce
1 cup sour cream (regular or light)

- Combine lime juice, peel, garlic, oil, salt and tequila. Rub into surface of tenderloin. Place pork, along with any extra marinade, in a plastic bag. Seal bag and allow to marinate 1 hour in refrigerator.

- Place wire rack in bowl of oven. Preheat oven to 500°F.

- Reduce oven heat to 425°F. Place pork directly on wire rack. Cook for 15 to 20 minutes or until meat thermometer registers 160°. Turn oven off and allow pork to sit in oven for 5 minutes.

- Combine enchilada sauce and sour cream in a saucepan. Heat until just warm. Remove pork from oven and slice into ½-inch medallions. Serve immediately with sauce.

Spicy Pork Saté

Cooking time: 6 to 8 minutes
Marinate: 1 hour or overnight

1 pound pork tenderloin; cut into 3-inch long, ½-inch wide, ¼ inch thick strips.

Marinade:

2 tablespoons Oriental sesame oil

¼ cup dry sherry

2 tablespoons soy sauce

2 tablespoons lime juice

1½ teaspoons garlic, minced

1 tablespoon finely minced fresh ginger or 1 teaspoon ground

Peanut Sauce:

½ cup smooth peanut butter (do not use old-fashioned or freshly ground)

1 cup low salt canned chicken broth

2 teaspoons Oriental sesame oil

½ cup chopped scallions

1 teaspoon garlic, minced

1 tablespoon lime juice

1 tablespoon brown sugar

1 teaspoon minced fresh ginger or ½ teaspoon ground

2 tablespoons hot sauce

1 tablespoon soy sauce

- In a large baking dish (do not use aluminum) combine the sesame oil, sherry, soy sauce, lime juice, garlic and ginger. Add the pork strips and toss to coat. Marinate in refrigerator 1 hour or overnight.

- In a blender or food processor whirl the peanut butter, broth, sesame oil, scallions, garlic, lime juice, brown sugar, ginger, hot sauce and soy sauce until smooth. Pour through a strainer into a medium saucepan. Simmer about 5 minutes or until thickened.

- Place upper rack into bowl of oven. Preheat oven to 500°F.

- Thread 9 to 10 pieces of pork onto each of four metal skewers. Keep oven heat at 500°F. Grill the pork skewers 6 to 8 minutes, turning once. Serve with peanut sauce.

HAM AND PINEAPPLE KABOBS WITH CHUTNEY CURRY GLAZE

Makes 4 Servings

Cooking time: 7 to 8 minutes

1 pound fully cooked smoked ham, cut into 1-inch chunks
20-ounce can pineapple chunks
⅓ cup mango chutney
⅓ cup juice from pineapple
½ teaspoon curry powder

■ Place upper rack into bowl of oven. Preheat oven to 500°F.

■ Alternate ham chunks and pineapple chunks on four metal skewers.

■ In blender or food processor whirl chutney, juice and curry powder until smooth. Brush kabobs with chutney glaze.

■ Keep oven heat at 500°F. Cook kabobs 4 minutes. Brush with glaze. Turn kabobs and cook 3 to 4 more minutes. Serve hot.

VEAL CHOPS STUFFED WITH SPINACH AND THREE CHEESES

Makes 6 Servings

Cooking time: 15 to 20 minutes

10 ounces frozen spinach, defrosted and squeezed dry

2 tablespoons dried minced onion or ¼ cup fresh onion

½ cup shredded Monterey Jack cheese

½ cup ricotta cheese

⅓ cup pepper feta cheese or plain feta

1 teaspoon coarsely ground black pepper

6 loin or rib veal chops, cut 1½ inches thick

■ Place wire rack into bowl of oven. Preheat oven to 500°F.

■ Combine spinach, onion, cheeses and pepper in a small bowl. Set aside. Make a deep slit about 3 inches long in the side of each veal chop to form a pocket. Do not cut all the way through the chop. Place about ¼ cup of stuffing into each chop. Close opening with toothpicks.

■ Reduce oven heat to 425°F. Place chops directly on wire rack and cook 15 to 20 minutes.

NOTE: Any leftover stuffing is great used to stuff vegetables or spread on French bread and placed under a hot broiler until bubbly.

ROASTED VEAL LOIN WITH GARLIC AND THYME

Makes 6 Servings

Cooking time: 50 to 60 minutes

3 pound boneless veal loin
2 teaspoons garlic, minced
1 tablespoon chopped fresh thyme or 1 teaspoon dried
Salt and pepper to taste
1 tablespoon olive oil

- Place wire rack into bowl of oven. Preheat oven to 500°F.

- With a sharp knife make deep slits every 3 inches down the length of the roast. Fill slits with garlic and thyme. Season loin with salt and pepper.

- Lay a 14x28-inch sheet of foil on a flat work surface. Place veal roast in center of foil. Brush veal with olive oil. Wrap foil neatly around veal.

- Reduce oven heat to 425°F. Place wrapped roast on wire rack and cook 50 to 60 minutes or until a meat thermometer reaches 170°. Allow roast to rest 10 minutes out of oven before slicing and serving.

VEAL CHOPS IN ORANGE BASIL SAUCE

Makes 4 Servings

Cooking time: 8 minutes

¾ cup orange juice
½ cup dry white wine
¼ cup minced scallions (white parts only)
½ cup heavy cream
4 ¾-inch thick rib veal chops

Salt and pepper to taste
4 tablespoons butter or margarine, melted
2 tablespoons chopped fresh basil or 2 teaspoons dry
½ teaspoon orange rind, grated

- Combine orange juice, wine and scallions in a small saucepan. Boil sauce to reduce to 3 tablespoons, about 10 minutes. Add cream, boil 1 minute.

- Place upper rack into bowl of oven. Preheat oven to 500°F.

- Sprinkle veal with salt and pepper. Keeping heat at 500°F, cook veal 4 minutes per side or until browned and cooked through. Reheat sauce and whisk in the butter or margarine. Stir in basil and orange peel. Serve surrounded with sauce.

GRILLED RIB LAMB CHOPS WITH WILTED GREENS

Makes 4 Servings

Cooking time: 6 to 10 minutes
Marinate: 1 to 3 hours

Marinade:

1 tablespoon Dijon mustard

1 tablespoon balsamic vinegar

1 garlic clove, minced

Salt and pepper to taste

⅓ cup olive oil

2 tablespoons chopped fresh basil leaves or 2 teaspoons dried

8 small rib lamb chops

¼ cup olive oil

1 garlic clove, minced

1 teaspoon hot sauce

1 head red leaf lettuce, coarsely chopped

2 Belgian endives, sliced crosswise in ¼-inch slices

Salt and pepper to taste

- In a small bowl (do not use aluminum) whisk the mustard, vinegar, garlic, salt and pepper. Slowly whisk in the olive oil, then add the basil. Arrange the chops in a glass or ceramic dish and pour the marinade on top. Turn to coat. Cover and marinate the chops for 1 to 3 hours, turning every 30 minutes.

- Place upper rack into bowl of oven. Preheat oven to 500°F.

- Remove chops from marinade. Reduce oven heat to 475°F. Cook the chops 6 to 10 minutes.

- While chops cook prepare wilted greens. In a large frying pan, heat the olive oil over low heat. Add the garlic and hot sauce. Cook 2 minutes. Add the lettuce and endive. Increase the heat to high and toss the greens 2 to 3 minutes or until wilted. Season with salt and pepper. Serve chops immediately with greens alongside.

LOIN LAMB CHOPS WITH TOMATOES AND ONIONS

Makes 2 Servings

Cooking time: 10-12 minutes

2   1¼-inch thick loin lamb chops

2 tablespoons olive oil

Salt and pepper to taste

1 teaspoon garlic

1 onion, sliced thin

½ teaspoon dried marjoram

1 tablespoon red wine vinegar

1 tablespoon balsamic vinegar

½ cup beef broth

¼ cup peeled and seeded plum tomatoes, chopped

1 tablespoon chopped fresh parsley

- Place wire rack into bowl of oven. Preheat oven to 500°F.

- Brush chops lightly with 1 tablespoon olive oil. Season with salt and pepper.

- Reduce oven heat to 475°F. Cook the chops 8 to 10 minutes.

- While chops cook, prepare sauce. In a medium frying pan cook the garlic and onion in remaining olive oil. Add the marjoram. Cook until onion is golden. Stir in vinegars and broth. Continue cooking and stirring until sauce thickens.

- Add the tomato and parsley. Top with the grilled chops. Cook and turn the chops for 2 minutes. Serve immediately with sauce.

LAMB MARINATED IN THYME AND LEMON

Makes 4 Servings

Cooking time: 8 to 10 minutes
Marinate: 30 minutes to 1 hour

¼ cup olive oil

2 teaspoons dried thyme leaves, crumbled

2 teaspoons lemon rind, grated

1 tablespoon fresh lemon juice

1 teaspoon pink peppercorns, crushed

4 loin lamb chops

½ teaspoon salt

- Combine the oil, thyme, lemon peel, lemon juice and peppercorns in a glass baking dish. Add the chops, turn to coat with marinade and cover. Refrigerate 30 minutes to 1 hour.

- Place upper rack into bowl of oven. Preheat oven to 500°F.

- Reduce oven heat to 475°F. Remove chops from marinade and cook them for 8 to 10 minutes. Season with salt and serve immediately.

Basil Garlic Shrimp and
Scallops en Brochette, *p.111*

FISH & SHELLFISH

Top Left:
Red Snapper Fillets with Olives, *p.108*

Top Right:
Grouper with Chili-Corn Sauce, *p.107*

Bottom:
Swordfish with Sun-Dried Tomatoes and Roasted Yellow Peppers, *p.103*

Basil Garlic Shrimp and
Scallops en Brochette, *p.111*

Top Left:
Red Snapper Fillets with Olives, *p.108*

Top Right:
Grouper with Chili-Corn Sauce, *p.107*

Bottom:
Swordfish with Sun-Dried Tomatoes and Roasted Yellow Peppers, *p.103*

Top Left:
Cajun Shrimp, p. 110

Top Right:
Pecan Crusted Snapper
Fillets with Lime Butter,
p. 100

Bottom:
Salmon Steaks with
Mustard Dill Sauce, p. 101

Fish Plates:
Tuna Teriyaki for Two, *p.105*

Left:
**Salmon Fillets in Tomato
Caper Sauce,** *p.104*

FISH & SHELLFISH

Seafood should be called God's food because it's so healthy and so incredibly tempting. With your Countertop Convection Oven and this cookbook, seafood is even more of a treat.

Try the **Flounder with Shiitake Mushrooms and Black Beans** and you'll know what I mean. Or the **Salmon Steaks with Mustard Dill Sauce.** Serve them to family and company for rave reviews.

Want to try something different? Then make **Grilled Sea Scallops in Cranberry Grapefruit Sauce.** They're sure to please the discerning palate. One of my favorites is **Roasted Monkfish with Onions, Herbs and Spices.** People tell me monkfish is a substitute for lobster. Well I believe monkfish has a taste all its own, especially when it's cooked using this special recipe.

Recently I served **Red Snapper Fillets with Olives** at a luncheon. Everyone said I should open a restaurant and serve this as the main entree for a four star rating. Maybe they're right, but I wouldn't stop there with so many wonderful seafood recipes at my disposal.

FLOUNDER STUFFED WITH CRABMEAT

Cooking time: 15 to 20 minutes

3 tablespoons butter or margarine

2 tablespoons finely chopped onion

2 tablespoons finely chopped green pepper

1½ cups lump crabmeat, checked for shells and cartilage

¾ cup mayonnaise

½ teaspoon white wine Worcestershire sauce

Salt and pepper to taste

8 small flounder fillets

- Place wire rack into bowl of oven. Preheat oven to 500°F. Grease a 9-inch metal baking pan.

- In a small skillet melt 2 tablespoons butter or margarine. Saute onion and green pepper until tender.

- Place crab in a small bowl. Add onion, green pepper, mayonnaise, Worcestershire sauce, salt and pepper. Mix gently to blend.

- Lay 4 fillets in the baking dish. Top each fillet with ¼ of the crab mixture. Top crab with another fillet. Melt the remaining tablespoon of butter or margarine and brush over fillets. Cover with foil.

- Reduce oven heat to 425°F. Bake fish 10 to 15 minutes or until it is opaque and flakes easily. Remove foil. Increase oven heat to 475°F and bake for 5 minutes or until nicely browned. Serve hot with tartar sauce and lemon wedges.

JALAPENO GLAZED HALIBUT

Makes 2 Servings

Cooking time: 10 to 15 minutes

2 teaspoons vegetable oil

¼ cup jalapeno jelly

1 teaspoon lemon or lime juice

2 6-ounce halibut fillets

Salt and pepper to taste

- Place wire rack into bowl of oven. Preheat oven to 500°F.

- Coat the bottom of a 9-inch nonstick coated metal baking pan with oil. Combine the jelly and lemon or lime juice. Brush fillets liberally with jelly mixture. Place fillets into pan.

- Reduce oven heat to 425°F. Cook fillets 10 to 15 minutes or until cooked through and fish flakes easily with a fork. Salt and pepper to taste.

SEAFOOD WITH DILL CHIVE BUTTER SAUCE

Makes 4 Servings

Cooking time: 6 to 10 minutes

1 package Hollandaise sauce mix
1 tablespoon lemon juice
1 tablespoon chopped fresh chives or 1 teaspoon dried
1 tablespoon chopped fresh dill or 1 teaspoon dried
¼ pound salmon fillet, cut into ¾-inch chunks
¼ pound small shrimp, shelled and deveined
¼ pound sea scallops, cut in half
1 lobster tail - meat removed and cut into ¾-inch chunks

- Place wire rack into bowl of oven. Preheat oven to 500°F.

- Prepare sauce mix according to package directions. Stir in lemon juice, chives and dill. Pour into a 9-inch metal baking dish. Add seafood.

- Reduce oven heat to 450°F. Bake for 5 to 7 minutes or until seafood is cooked through.

THE BEST CUT OF FISH, THE CENTER CUT, IS NORMALLY RICHER IN FLAVOR AND IS A MORE TENDER CUT THAN A PIECE FROM THE TAIL OF THE FISH.

✔ *Check your owner's manual for preheating time which may vary by manufacturer.*

FLOUNDER WITH PIMIENTO PUREE

Makes 2 Servings

Cooking time: 7 to 9 minutes

1 teaspoon vegetable oil

1 teaspoon butter or margarine

4 scallions, white part only, chopped

4 small flounder fillet halves (about 3 ounces each)

1 tablespoon lime juice

Salt and pepper

1½-ounces jarred pimientos

½ teaspoon garlic, minced

½ teaspoon Oriental sesame oil

■ Place wire rack into bowl of oven. Preheat oven to 500°F.

■ Put oil and butter or margarine into a 9-inch nonstick coated metal baking pan.

■ Reduce oven heat to 425°F. Place pan on wire rack and allow butter to melt (about 1 minute). Add scallions to pan and cook for 2 to 3 minutes.

■ Season flounder with lime juice, salt and pepper. Place in pan with scallions. Cook 5 to 6 minutes or until opaque and fish flakes easily with a fork.

■ In a blender or food processor puree the pimiento with the garlic and sesame oil.

■ When fish is done, place on serving plate and keep warm. Add puree to pan juices and stir to combine. Cook puree and juices in the oven about 2 minutes to blend all flavors. Serve fish surrounded with sauce.

PECAN CRUSTED SNAPPER FILLETS WITH LIME BUTTER

Makes 4 Servings

Cooking time: 9 to 10 minutes

1 cup lowfat sour cream

1½ cups chopped pecans

4   6-ounce snapper fillets

Lime Butter:

4 tablespoons unsalted butter, softened

2 teaspoons lime juice

Grated rind of 1 lime

■ Spray rack with cooking spray. Place wire rack into bowl of oven. Preheat oven to 500°F.

■ Spread sour cream and nuts on two separate plates. Coat fish fillets first with sour cream, then nuts. Place fillets directly on wire rack.

- Reduce oven heat to 425°F. Bake 9 to 10 minutes until fish flakes easily with a fork.

- While fish cooks, make lime butter. Combine butter, juice and rind until well blended. When fish is done, top each fillet with about 1 tablespoon of butter mixture. Remove from oven just when butter begins to melt.

SALMON STEAKS WITH MUSTARD DILL SAUCE

Makes 4 Servings

Cooking time: 7 to 10 minutes

4 salmon steaks, cut 1-inch thick
1 package Hollandaise sauce
1 tablespoon lemon juice
1 tablespoon Dijon mustard
1 tablespoon chopped fresh
dill or 1 teaspoon dried

- Place upper rack into bowl of oven. Preheat oven to 500°F.

- Keep heat at 500°F. Place salmon in 9-inch baking pan and cook for 7 to 10 minutes or until fish flakes easily with a fork.

- While salmon cooks, prepare Hollandaise sauce according to package directions. When done, whisk in lemon juice, mustard and dill. Serve salmon surrounded with sauce.

SNAPPER IN TARRAGON LIME SAUCE

Makes 4 Servings

Cooking time: 6 to 10 minutes

1 package Bearnaise sauce
2 teaspoons lime juice
1 teaspoon vegetable oil
4   6-ounce snapper fillets
Salt and pepper to taste
2 teaspoons fresh tarragon or ½ teaspoon dried

- Place upper rack into bowl of oven. Preheat oven to 500°F.

- Prepare Bearnaise sauce according to package directions. Stir in 1 teaspoon lime juice at the end of cooking. Set aside.

- Combine remaining lime juice and vegetable oil. Brush on fish fillets. Season fillets with salt and pepper. Place in 9-inch metal baking pan.

- Reduce oven heat to 475°F. Cook fish 6 to 10 minutes or until fish flakes easily with a fork.

- Gently reheat sauce. Surround snapper with sauce and sprinkle with tarragon.

FLOUNDER WITH SHIITAKE MUSHROOMS AND BLACK BEANS

Makes 2 Servings

Cooking time: 9 to 11 minutes

1 tablespoon Oriental black beans
¼ pound shiitake mushrooms, thinly sliced
½ teaspoon garlic, minced
1 tablespoon soy sauce
½ teaspoon Oriental sesame oil
1 tablespoon dry sherry
1 tablespoon grated fresh ginger or
1 teaspoon ground
1 teaspoon rice wine vinegar
4 small flounder fillets (about 3-ounces each)
1 teaspoon vegetable oil

- Place upper rack into bowl of oven. Preheat oven to 500°F.

- Drain and rinse the black beans. Chop.

- Place the black beans, shiitakes, garlic, soy sauce, sesame oil, sherry, ginger and vinegar in a 9-inch metal baking pan. Toss all ingredients to blend.

- Reduce oven heat to 425°F. Cook shiitake mixture 3 to 4 minutes. Brush fillets with the vegetable oil. Place fillets atop the shiitake mixture and cook 6 to 7 minutes or until fish flakes easily with a fork. Serve fillets with shiitake mixture spooned over them.

SWORDFISH WITH SUN-DRIED TOMATOES AND ROASTED YELLOW PEPPERS

Makes 4 Servings

Cooking time: 15 to 20 minutes

1 tablespoon olive oil
1 large red onion, thinly sliced
2 large yellow peppers, cut into 1½ x ¼-inch strips
2 garlic cloves, minced
1 teaspoon fresh thyme or ⅛ teaspoon dry
¼ teaspoon salt
Freshly ground black pepper
2 tablespoons oil-packed, sun-dried tomatoes, drained and chopped
1 tablespoon balsamic vinegar
½ cup white wine
4 6-ounce swordfish fillets

- Place wire rack into bowl of oven. Preheat oven to 500°F.

- Coat bottom of a 9-inch baking pan with the oil. Add the onions, peppers and garlic. Sprinkle with thyme, salt and pepper.

- Reduce oven heat to 450°F. Cook the vegetables 5 minutes or until they begin to brown. Remove pan from oven.

- Add to the pan the sun-dried tomatoes, vinegar, wine and swordfish. Cover the pan tightly with foil and return to oven. Cook 15 minutes or until fish is cooked through and flakes easily. Serve fish with vegetables and juices.

SALMON FILLETS IN TOMATO CAPER SAUCE

Makes 2 Servings°

Cooking time: 25 minutes

2 6-ounce salmon fillets

1 tablespoon vegetable oil

Salt and pepper to taste

1 tablespoon butter or margarine

2 scallions, chopped, white part only

½ teaspoon garlic, minced

1 cup crushed tomatoes

1 tablespoon capers

■ Place wire rack into bowl of oven. Preheat oven to 500°F.

■ Brush fillets with oil. Season with salt and pepper. Set aside.

■ In a 9-inch metal baking pan, combine the butter or margarine, scallions and garlic. Reduce oven heat to 425°F. Cook the scallion mixture for 5 minutes.

■ Stir in the tomatoes and capers. Cook 3 minutes. Top mixture with salmon. Cook another 20 minutes or until fish flakes easily with a fork. Spoon sauce on serving plate and top with fish.

BROILED GROUPER WITH MINT AND GARLIC

Makes 4 Servings

Cooking time: 9 to 11 minutes

4 6-ounce grouper fillets

1 tablespoon vegetable oil

Salt and pepper to taste

¼ cup butter or margarine

½ cup packed fresh mint leaves, minced

2 teaspoons garlic, chopped

■ Place wire rack into bowl of oven. Preheat oven to 500°F.

■ Brush fillets with oil. Season with salt and pepper. Place fillets in 9-inch metal baking pan.

■ Reduce oven heat to 475°F. Cook fish 9 to 11 minutes or until fish is opaque and flakes easily with a fork.

■ While fish cooks, make sauce. In a small saucepan, heat the butter or margarine over medium heat until foamy. Add the mint and garlic. Cook and stir for about one minute. Keep warm. When fish is done place on serving dish and pour sauce over fish.

GRILLED MONKFISH WITH MUSTARD PARSLEY SAUCE

Makes 4 Servings

Cooking time: 7 to 9 minutes

2 tablespoons white wine vinegar

2 tablespoons grainy mustard

3 tablespoons fresh parsley, coarsely chopped

⅜ cup olive oil

4 6-ounce monkfish fillets, 1-inch thick

1 tablespoon vegetable oil

- Place upper rack into bowl of oven. Preheat oven to 500°F.

- In a blender or food processor whirl the vinegar, mustard and parsley. With the motor running, add the olive oil in a thin stream, blend until sauce is emulsified.

- Brush both sides of monkfish with vegetable oil. Place in 9-inch metal baking pan. Cook at 500°F for 7 to 9 minutes until fish flakes easily with a fork.

- Place monkfish on serving platter. Pour sauce over fish and serve.

TUNA TERIYAKI FOR TWO

Makes 2 Servings

Cooking time: 7 to 9 minutes
Marinate: 30 minutes

2 tablespoons teriyaki sauce or soy sauce

2 scallions, chopped

½ teaspoon ground ginger

2 6-ounce tuna steaks

2 teaspoons peanut oil or vegetable oil

½ cup water

1 teaspoon cornstarch dissolved in 1 tablespoon water

- Combine teriyaki or soy sauce, scallions and ginger in a shallow glass baking dish. Add tuna and turn once to coat with sauce. Cover dish and refrigerate 30 minutes.

- Place upper rack into bowl of oven. Preheat oven to 500°F.

- Remove tuna from marinade. Reserve marinade for sauce. Brush both sides of tuna steaks with oil. Reduce oven heat to 475°F and cook steaks 7 to 9 minutes or until desired degree of doneness.

- While tuna cooks make sauce. Transfer marinade to a small saucepan. Add water to pan. On stovetop burner over high heat, bring sauce to a boil. Boil for 1 minute. Stir in dissolved cornstarch. Reduce heat, simmer and stir for 3 minutes.

- Place tuna on serving plates. Pour sauce over tuna and serve.

ROASTED MONKFISH WITH ONIONS, HERBS AND SPICES

Cooking time: 9 to 12 minutes

2 tablespoons olive oil

1 medium onion, sliced thin

2 teaspoons garlic, minced

2 tablespoons chopped fresh parsley or 2 teaspoons dry

2 teaspoons paprika

1 teaspoon hot sauce

Pinch of dried thyme

2 teaspoons white wine vinegar

4   6 to 7-ounce monkfish fillets

- Place wire rack into bowl of oven. Preheat oven to 500°F.
- Pour 1 tablespoon olive oil into 9-inch metal baking pan.
- Cook onion and garlic in a small frying pan in remaining olive oil. Add the parsley, paprika, hot sauce, thyme and vinegar.
- Reduce oven heat to 425°F. Heat the pan with the oil in the oven for 1 minute. Add the fish to the pan. Top with onion/spice mixture. Bake for 9 to 12 minutes or until fish flakes easily with a fork.

BAKED TUNA OR SWORDFISH WITH WHITE BEANS AND GARLIC

Makes 2 Servings

Cooking time: 15 to 20 minutes

10 ounces canned Cannelloni beans (white kidney beans), drained and rinsed

1 teaspoon garlic, minced

2 tablespoons olive oil

2 tablespoons chopped fresh parsley or 2 teaspoons dried

Salt and pepper to taste

2   6-ounce tuna or swordfish steaks

- Place upper rack into bowl of oven. Preheat oven to 500°F.
- Combine beans, garlic, 1 tablespoon olive oil, parsley, salt and pepper in a 9-inch metal baking pan.
- Brush fish with remaining olive oil. Place fish atop beans. Cover pan with foil.
- Reduce oven heat to 425°F. Cook fish and beans 15 to 20 minutes or until fish flakes easily with a fork and beans are hot.

Bluefish Fillets with Lemon Chive Caper Sauce

Makes 2 Servings

Cooking time: 8 to 10 minutes

2 6-ounce skinless bluefish fillets

2 tablespoons unsalted butter or margarine

1 tablespoon lemon juice

1 tablespoon chopped fresh chives or 1 teaspoon dried

1 tablespoon capers, drained

■ Spray upper rack with cooking spray. Place upper rack into bowl of oven. Preheat oven to 500°F.

■ Reduce oven heat to 475°F. Place fillets in 9-inch metal baking pan and cook for 8 to 10 minutes or until fish flakes easily with a fork.

■ While fish is cooking, in a small saucepan melt the butter or margarine until foamy. Stir in the lemon juice, chives and capers. Serve sauce over fish.

Grouper with Chili-Corn Sauce

Makes 4 Servings

Cooking time: 8 to 10 minutes

4 6-ounce grouper fillets

2 tablespoons olive oil

2 jalapeno chilies, seeded and minced

2 teaspoons scallions, chopped (white part only)

1 teaspoon garlic, minced

1 tablespoon chili powder

⅛ teaspoon cumin

1 cup heavy cream

2 cups corn kernels

Salt and pepper to taste

2 teaspoons fresh lemon juice

■ Place upper rack into bowl of oven. Preheat oven to 500°F.

■ Reduce oven heat to 475°F. Brush grouper with 1 tablespoon oil. Place in 9-inch metal baking pan and cook 8 to 10 minutes or until fish flakes easily with a fork.

■ While fish is cooking, heat remaining olive oil in a medium saucepan over medium heat. Add chilies, scallions and garlic. Saute 2 minutes. Mix in chili powder, cumin, cream and corn. Cook until sauce thickens, stirring occasionally, about 5 minutes. Season with salt, pepper and lemon juice. Spoon sauce on plates and top with fillets.

BROILED COD FILLETS WITH TOMATO BUTTER SAUCE

Makes 4 Servings

Cooking time: 10 to 12 minutes

1 tablespoon red onion, chopped

¼ cup white wine

4   6-ounce cod fillets, ¾- to 1-inch thick

1 tablespoon vegetable oil

1 teaspoon lemon juice

¼ cup cold unsalted butter or margarine, cut into bits

2 plum tomatoes, seeded and chopped

2 tablespoons chopped fresh parsley or 2 teaspoons dried

Salt and pepper to taste

- ■ Place upper rack into bowl of oven. Preheat oven to 500°F.
- ■ In a small saucepan simmer onion and wine until reduced to a tablespoon.
- ■ Brush both sides of cod fillets with vegetable oil. Place fillets in 9-inch metal pan.
- ■ Reduce oven heat to 475°F. Cook for 8 to 10 minutes or until fish flakes easily with a fork.
- ■ While fish cooks, reheat wine and onion mixture. Add lemon juice. Whisk in butter or margarine one piece at a time. Add tomatoes. Stir gently just until tomatoes are heated. Toss in parsley, salt and pepper. Serve fillets surrounded with sauce.

RED SNAPPER FILLETS WITH OLIVES

Makes 4 Servings

Cooking time: 9 to 11 minutes

2 tablespoons olive oil

½ teaspoon chopped garlic, minced

½ cup black olives

¼ cup green pimiento stuffed olives, chopped

1 teaspoon dried oregano

1 teaspoon dried basil

¼ cup lemon juice

2 tablespoons chopped fresh parsley or 2 teaspoons dried

4   6-ounce red snapper fillets

Salt and pepper to taste

- Place wire rack into bowl of oven. Preheat oven to 500°F.

- Pour olive oil into a 9-inch metal baking pan.

- In a small bowl stir together garlic, black olives, green olives, oregano, basil, lemon juice and parsley. Season the fillets with salt and pepper.

- Reduce oven heat to 425°F. Pour the olive/garlic sauce into the pan. Cook 1 minute. Top with snapper fillets and spoon some sauce on top. Bake for 9 to 11 minutes or until fillets flake easily with a fork.

TUNA MARGARITA WITH MUSTARD SAUCE

Makes 2 Servings

Cooking time: 7 to 9 minutes
Marinate: 1 hour

Juice and grated rind of 1 lime
⅓ cup tequila
1 teaspoon coarse salt
½ teaspoon coarsely ground pepper
2 6-ounce tuna steaks
½ of a package of Hollandaise sauce mix
3 tablespoons grainy mustard

- In a glass baking dish or pie plate, combine the lime juice, rind, tequila, salt and pepper. Place fish in mixture and turn to coat. Cover and refrigerate one hour.

- Prepare Hollandaise sauce (½ of a package) according to package directions. Stir in mustard. Set aside.

- Place upper rack into bowl of oven. Preheat oven to 500°F.

- Reduce oven heat to 475°F. Remove tuna from marinade and place in 9-inch metal baking pan. Cook 7 to 9 minutes or until fish flakes easily with a fork.

- Gently reheat sauce. Spread sauce into a circle on each serving plate. Top sauce with a tuna steak.

SALMON AND SWORDFISH NUGGETS IN GRAPEFRUIT BUTTER

Cooking time: 8 to 10 minutes

6-ounce skinless swordfish steak, cut into 1½-inch pieces

6-ounce skinless salmon fillet, cut into 1½-inch pieces

¼ cup grapefruit juice

Salt and pepper to taste

Grated rind of ½ grapefruit

1½ tablespoons butter

■ Place wire rack into bowl of oven. Preheat oven to 500°F.

■ Arrange fish pieces in a 9-inch metal baking pan. Drizzle fish with grapefruit juice. Season with salt and pepper. Sprinkle with rind.

■ Reduce oven heat to 425°F. Cook until opaque and fish flakes easily with a fork - 8 to 10 minutes. Remove fish to a serving dish and keep warm.

■ Transfer pan juices to a small saucepan. Cook juices over high heat until reduced by half. Swirl in the butter. Pour sauce over fish.

CAJUN SHRIMP

Makes 4 Servings

Cooking time: 10 minutes
Marinate: 1 hour

¼ cup olive oil

2 tablespoons Cajun seasoning

1 tablespoon hot sauce

2 tablespoons fresh lime juice

1 teaspoon garlic, minced

1 tablespoon brown sugar

1 pound uncooked large shrimp, shelled and deveined

Cooked rice

■ In a 9-inch baking pan (do not use aluminum) combine oil, cajun seasoning, hot sauce, lime juice, garlic and brown sugar. Add shrimp and coat with sauce. Cover and refrigerate 1 hour.

■ Place wire rack into bowl of oven. Preheat oven to 500°F.

■ Reduce oven heat to 425°F. If using a glass dish place a piece of foil the same size as the baking dish directly on the wire rack. Place baking dish with shrimp on foil. Bake for 10 minutes, occasionally lift oven top and stir, until shrimp turn pink. Serve hot over rice.

BASIL GARLIC SHRIMP AND SCALLOPS EN BROCHETTE

Makes 4 Servings

Cooking time: 8 minutes
Marinate: 2 hours in refrigerator

¼ cup olive oil

1 tablespoon lemon juice

¼ cup white wine

1 tablespoon chopped fresh basil or 1 teaspoon dried

1 teaspoon garlic, minced

1 teaspoon salt

1 pound sea scallops

1 pound medium shrimp, peeled and deveined

■ Combine oil, lemon juice, wine, basil, garlic and salt in 9x13-inch glass baking dish. Add scallops and shrimp. Toss to coat with marinade. Cover and refrigerate 2 hours.

■ Place upper rack into bowl of oven. Preheat oven to 500°F.

■ Alternate marinated shrimp and scallops on metal skewers. Save marinade.

■ Keep oven heat at 500°F. Cook skewers for 4 minutes, then brush with reserved marinade. Cook 4 or 5 minutes longer or until shrimp has turned pink and scallops are slightly browned.

ROASTED CRAB CAKES

Makes 4

Cooking time: 10 to 15 minutes

2 cups crabmeat, checked for shells and cartilage

1 teaspoon Dijon mustard

½ cup mayonnaise

1 teaspoon lemon juice

2 teaspoons minced fresh parsley

¾ cup dry bread crumbs

4 tablespoons melted butter or margarine

■ Place wire rack into bowl of oven. Preheat oven to 500°F.

■ Mix crabmeat, mustard, mayonnaise, lemon juice and parsley together. Form into 4 cakes.

■ Spread bread crumbs on a large plate. Gently pat cakes with crumbs to coat. Place cakes in a 9-inch metal baking pan. Drizzle with melted butter or margarine.

■ Reduce oven heat to 350°F. Bake cakes 10 to 15 minutes or until heated through and nicely browned.

LEMON SCALLOPS WITH QUICK ROUILLE

Makes 2 Servings

Cooking time: 4 to 6 minutes
Marinate: 30 minutes

Rouille:

3 ounces pimientos, drained

½ cup mayonnaise

1 slice firm white bread, torn up

1 teaspoon garlic, minced

1 tablespoon hot sauce

1 tablespoon olive oil

1 tablespoon lemon juice

1 teaspoon chopped garlic, minced

Salt and pepper to taste

1 pound sea scallops

■ Make rouille by combining pimientos, mayonnaise, bread, garlic and hot sauce in blender or food processor. Whirl until creamy. Pour into small bowl. Cover and refrigerate.

■ In a baking dish, combine olive oil, lemon juice, garlic, salt and pepper. Add scallops. Toss to coat. Cover and refrigerate for 30 minutes.

■ Place upper rack into bowl of oven. Preheat oven to 500°F.

■ Remove scallops from marinade. Place in a 9-inch metal baking pan.

■ Cook at 500°F for 4 to 6 minutes or until opaque and lightly browned. Serve with dollop of rouille.

GRILLED SEA SCALLOPS IN CRANBERRY GRAPEFRUIT SAUCE

Makes 4 Servings

Cooking time: 10 minutes

½ cup cranberries

1 tablespoon brown sugar, firmly packed

1 tablespoon grapefruit juice

Grated rind of ½ grapefruit

1 tablespoon of vermouth

1 tablespoon vegetable oil

1 tablespoon Sambuca liqueur (optional)

1 pound sea scallops

■ Place upper rack into bowl of oven. Preheat oven to 500°F.

■ In a small saucepan combine cranberries, brown sugar, grapefruit juice, rind and vermouth. Simmer 3 minutes or until cranberries pop. Set aside.

■ Coat a 9-inch metal baking pan with vegetable oil and Sambuca. In the baking pan toss the scallops with the vegetable oil and Sambuca. Keep oven heat at 500°F. Cook scallops 6 minutes or until opaque, stirring after 3 minutes. Remove scallops with slotted spoon. Arrange scallops on a serving platter. Pour any juice from pan into cranberry mixture. Boil sauce 1 minute until syrupy. Pour over scallops and serve.

Baked Acorn
Squash with
Sweet Potatoes
and Golden
Raisins, *p.123*

Top Left:
**Roasted New Potato
and Beet Salad with
Dill Dressing,** *p.118*

Middle:
**Green Beans with
Marjoram Butter,** *p.122*

Bottom:
Grecian Zucchini,
p.121

Top:
Roasted Brussels
Sprouts, p.132

Bottom:
Roasted Peppers,
Potatoes and
Green Beans, p.131

Left:
Baby Carrots in Lemon Mint Glaze, *p.129*

Right:
Sweet and Sour Braised Red Cabbage, *p.128*

Bottom:
**Baked Stuffed Tomatoes with
Mushrooms and Chives,** *p.124*

VEGETABLES

In this section, vegetables take on a new dimension and you will delight at the number of great recipes that await you. I know I could make a feast using just the vegetable recipes that follow.

Those who like beets will love **Beets and Honey Lemon Glaze**. If former President George Bush never tried **Broccoli, Corn and Pepper with Lime Butter**, maybe he should, because broccoli becomes a terrific dish when served this way.

Having visited many different areas of the country, I have found so many vegetable variations that it's hard to pick a favorite. Try the **Herb Crusted Zucchini**, the **Baby Carrots in Lemon Mint Glaze** or the **Baked Acorn Squash with Sweet Potatoes and Golden Raisins**. Each is so special! These recipes will reintroduce you to some old favorites in a whole new way.

CORN WITH PAPRIKA BUTTER

Cooking time: 15 minutes

1½ cups fresh or frozen corn kernels
2 tablespoons butter or margarine
1 tablespoon paprika
½ teaspoon seasoned salt

■ Place wire rack into bowl of oven. Preheat oven to 500°F.

■ Combine corn, butter or margarine, paprika and seasoned salt in a 9-inch baking pan. Cover pan with foil.

Reduce oven heat to 400°F. Cook corn for 15 minutes or until tender. Serve hot.

ROASTED NEW POTATO AND BEET SALAD WITH DILL DRESSING

Makes 4 to 6 Servings

Cooking time: 15 minutes

2 tablespoons olive oil
12 to 16 small new potatoes (about 4 cups), scrubbed and cut into 1-inch cubes
1-pound can whole, small beets, cut in 4 to 6 pieces

Dressing:
⅓ cup olive oil
⅓ cup red wine vinegar
1 teaspoon salt
½ teaspoon coarsely ground black pepper
¼ cup scallions, minced
2 tablespoons finely chopped fresh dill or 2 teaspoons dried

■ Place wire rack into bowl of oven. Preheat oven to 500°F.

■ Place olive oil in 9-inch metal baking pan. Add potatoes to pan and toss to coat with oil.

- Reduce oven heat to 400°F. Cook potatoes 15 minutes. Tossing every 5 minutes, making sure to bring unbrowned potatoes up from bottom.

- Transfer potatoes to a medium bowl. Add cut beets. Drizzle with oil and vinegar. Add salt, pepper, scallions and dill. Mix well. Allow to sit at room temperature for at least 30 minutes so flavors can combine. Serve slightly warm, at room temperature or chilled.

ROASTED FENNEL AND CELERY

Makes 4 Servings

Cooking time: 15 to 20 minutes

1 tablespoon butter or margarine, melted
1 tablespoon olive oil
2 cups fennel bulb, sliced into ½ x 3-inch slices
2½ cups celery, sliced into ½ x 3-inch slices
1 teaspoon fennel seeds
Salt and pepper to taste

- Place wire rack in bowl of oven. Preheat oven to 500°F.

- Coat a 9-inch metal baking pan with butter or margarine and oil. Add fennel, celery, fennel seed, salt and pepper. Toss to coat with butter or margarine and oil.

- Reduce oven heat to 350°F. Cook vegetables 15 to 20 minutes, stirring every 5 minutes, until tender. Serve hot.

FENNEL IS A EUROPEAN HERB OF THE CARROT FAMILY AND IS CULTIVATED FOR ITS AROMATIC SEEDS. YOU CAN FIND FENNEL IN MOST SUPERMARKETS IN THE PRODUCE SECTION.

✔ *Check your owner's manual for preheating time which may vary by manufacturer.*

HERB CRUSTED ZUCCHINI

Cooking time: 10 to 12 minutes

2 medium sized zucchini
½ cup dry bread crumbs
⅓ cup grated Parmesan cheese
2 tablespoons grated Romano cheese
2 teaspoons Italian seasoning
1 teaspoon garlic salt
¼ teaspoon black pepper
1 tablespoon olive oil

- Place wire rack into bowl of oven. Preheat oven to 500°F.

- Cut zucchini in half lengthwise, cut off and discard ends. Cut halves into 1½-inch chunks. Combine bread crumbs, cheeses, Italian seasoning, garlic salt and pepper.

- Pour olive oil into a bowl big enough to hold zucchini. Toss zucchini in oil to coat. Place crumb mixture onto a large flat plate. Roll zucchini in crumbs to coat.

- Place the coated zucchini into a 9-inch metal baking dish. Reduce oven heat to 375°F and bake 10 to 12 minutes until tender.

PEPPER BOATS WITH RICE AND BLACK BEANS

Cooking time: 20 to 25 minutes

2 large bell peppers (any color)
1 tablespoon olive oil
1 small onion, chopped
½ teaspoon garlic, minced
½ cup cooked rice
8-ounces canned black beans drained and rinsed

1 cup crushed tomatoes
½ teaspoon dried oregano
½ teaspoon ground cumin
1½ teaspoons chili powder
1 cup grated Monterey Jack cheese

- Place wire rack into bowl of oven. Preheat oven to 500°F.

- Halve the peppers lengthwise. Remove pulp, seeds and stem.

- Heat the oil in a large frying pan. Add onion and garlic. Saute until soft. Stir in the cooked rice, beans and ½ cup of the crushed tomatoes. Add the oregano, cumin and chili powder. Combine well. Stuff mixture into each pepper half. Spoon remaining ½ cup of crushed tomatoes over each pepper.

- Reduce oven heat to 375°F. Place peppers directly on wire rack. Bake for 15 to 20 minutes. Top each pepper with grated cheese. Continue baking 3 to 5 minutes. Serve with a little olive oil drizzled over the top if desired.

GRECIAN ZUCCHINI

Makes 4 Servings

Cooking time: 30 to 35 minutes

1 pound zucchini, scrubbed, trimmed and coarsely grated
3 scallions, chopped
1 egg
¼ cup chopped fresh parsley
¼ cup fresh mint or 4 teaspoons dried, crushed mint
¾ cup grated Gruyére cheese (about 4-ounces)
2-ounces feta cheese, crumbled
Pinch cayenne pepper or dash of hot sauce
Salt and pepper to taste
⅝ cup flour
½ cup fresh bread crumbs
¼ stick butter or margarine, cut into bits
10 small black olives
(preferably Mediterranean style brine-cured)

- Place wire rack into bowl of oven. Preheat oven to 500°F.

- In a large bowl stir together the zucchini, scallions, egg, parsley, mint, ½ cup of the Gruyére, feta and cayenne or hot sauce. Salt and pepper to taste. Add the flour gradually while stirring. Spread the mixture evenly in a greased 9-inch metal baking pan. Sprinkle with bread crumbs and remaining Gruyére. Dot with the butter or margarine and arrange the olives on top.

- Reduce oven heat to 400°F. Bake 5 minutes. Cover the pan securely with foil and continue baking 25 to 30 minutes.

GREEN BEANS WITH MARJORAM BUTTER

Makes 4 Servings

Cooking time: 12 to 15 minutes

2½ cups fresh whole green beans, washed and trimmed
2 teaspoons vegetable oil
2 tablespoons butter or margarine
1 teaspoon dried marjoram, crushed
Salt and pepper
1 cup boiling water

- Place wire rack into bowl of oven. Preheat oven to 500°F.
- Coat bottom of a 9-inch metal baking pan with oil.
- In a small saucepan melt butter or margarine. Add marjoram, salt and pepper. Take pan off heat. Allow flavors to blend while preparing beans.
- Place beans in heat-proof bowl or Pyrex measuring cup. Cover beans with boiling water. Allow to sit one minute. Drain. Arrange beans in pan and toss to coat with oil.
- Reduce oven heat to 425°F. Cook beans 12 to 15 minutes or until tender. Pour marjoram butter over beans. Toss to coat.

SUMMER VEGETABLE TORTE WITH PESTO AND RASPBERRY VINAIGRETTE

Makes 4 Servings

Cooking time: 30 minutes

1 tablespoon olive oil
1½ cups zucchini, sliced ¼-inch thick
4 Italian plum tomatoes, sliced ¼-inch thick
½ cup red onion, sliced thin
7-ounce container prepared pesto
1½ cups yellow squash, sliced ¼-inch thick

Raspberry Vinaigrette:
½ cup olive oil
¼ cup raspberry vinegar
½ teaspoon garlic, minced
Salt and pepper to taste

- Place wire rack into bowl of oven. Preheat oven to 500°F.
- Cover the bottom of a 9-inch metal baking pan with olive oil. Spread zucchini slices on bottom of baking dish. Top with some tomato and onion slices. Dot with some of the pesto. Make a layer of yellow squash, more tomatoes, onions and pesto. Continue layering until all ingredients are used. Cover pan securely with foil.
- Reduce oven heat to 325°F. Bake 30 minutes or until vegetables are just tender. Allow to cool to room temperature. Cover and chill torte overnight. Serve chilled or room temperature with raspberry vinaigrette.

Raspberry Vinaigrette:

- Combine all ingredients in a jar with a tight fitting lid. Shake jar to combine. Serve with vegetable torte.

BAKED ACORN SQUASH WITH SWEET POTATOES AND GOLDEN RAISINS

Makes 4 Servings

Cooking time: 35 to 45 minutes

1 acorn squash, ends removed
1 medium sweet potato or yam
¼ cup golden raisins
1 tablespoon brown sugar
Grated rind of 1 orange
¼ teaspoon nutmeg
2 tablespoons melted butter or margarine
Juice of one orange

- Place wire rack into bowl of oven. Preheat oven to 500°F.
- Slice squash into 4 rings. Remove seeds and any stringy material from squash rings. Wash and peel sweet potato. Cut into ½ x¼-inch pieces.
- Toss together sweet potato pieces, raisins, brown sugar, orange rind and nutmeg.
- Lay a 28x14-inch piece of foil on a work surface. Arrange squash on foil. Sprinkle with sweet potato mixture, butter or margarine and orange juice. Fold foil up in neat package.
- Reduce oven heat to 400°F. Place foil package directly on wire rack. Bake 35 to 45 minutes. Carefully open package to avoid being burned by steam. Arrange squash on serving platter. Top with potatoes and raisins. Pour juices over all.

BAKED STUFFED TOMATOES WITH MUSHROOMS AND CHIVES

Makes 4 Servings

Cooking time: 15 to 20 minutes

4 medium tomatoes

1 cup mushrooms, washed and sliced

½ cup chopped onion

2 tablespoons olive oil

2 tablespoons minced fresh parsley or 2 teaspoons dried

1 tablespoon finely minced fresh chives or 1 teaspoon dried

2 teaspoons dried oregano

Salt and pepper to taste

½ cup bread crumbs

- Grease an 8x8-inch metal baking pan.

- Slice thin layer off top of each tomato. Carefully scoop out pulp and reserve.

- Saute mushrooms and onions in olive oil. Add parsley, chives, oregano, salt and pepper. Stir in bread crumbs. Add enough reserved pulp to moisten mixture.

- Place wire rack into bowl of oven. Preheat oven to 500°F.

- Stuff tomatoes with bread crumb mixture. Arrange tomatoes in pan. Drizzle with olive oil.

- Reduce oven heat to 400°F. Bake for 15 to 20 minutes or until tender. Cover with foil if tomatoes are browning too quickly. Serve hot or at room temperature.

PEARL ONIONS BAKED IN CELERY SAUCE
Makes 3 to 4 Servings

Cooking time: 10 to 15 minutes

12¼-ounce jar pearl onions, drained and liquid reserved
½ can of condensed cream of celery soup
2 tablespoons chopped parsley
¼ cup bread crumbs
2 teaspoons melted butter or margarine

■ Place wire rack into bowl of oven. Preheat oven to 500°F.

■ Place drained onions in a greased 8-inch metal baking pan. In a small bowl blend the soup and reserved onion liquid and 1 tablespoon parsley. Pour over onions.

■ Toss together the bread crumbs and butter or margarine. Drizzle on top of onions and sauce. Cover pan with foil.

■ Reduce oven heat to 400°F and bake 10 to 15 minutes or until hot. Sprinkle with remaining parsley.

BEETS AND HONEY LEMON GLAZE
Makes 4 Servings

Cooking time: 10 minutes

16-ounce can sliced beets
1 tablespoon lemon juice
¼ cup honey
2 teaspoons butter or margarine

■ Grease a 9-inch metal baking pan.

■ Place wire rack into bowl of oven. Preheat oven to 500°F.

■ Place beets, lemon juice, honey and butter or margarine in pan.

■ Reduce oven heat to 425°F. Cook beets 10 minutes or until heated through. Occasionally lift oven top and stir beets to coat with glaze.

CREAMY SPINACH GRATIN

Makes 4 Servings

Cooking time: 20 minutes

¼ cup buttermilk baking mix (such as Bisquick)

1 egg

½ cup milk

10-ounce package frozen spinach, thawed and drained

4-ounces lowfat cream cheese, softened

*¼ cup fresh chopped onion or
2 tablespoons minced dried*

⅛ teaspoon nutmeg

½ teaspoon salt

½ teaspoon pepper

¼ cup grated Parmesan

- Grease an 8x8-inch metal baking pan.

- Place wire rack into bowl of oven. Preheat oven to 500°F.

- In a small bowl blend the baking mix, egg and milk. Stir in the spinach, cream cheese, onion, nutmeg, salt and pepper. Pour mixture into pan.

- Reduce oven heat to 350°F. Bake gratin 15 minutes. Sprinkle with Parmesan cheese and bake 5 minutes more.

CAULIFLOWER IN MUSTARD CREAM SAUCE

Makes 2 Servings

Cooking time: 10 to 15 minutes

8-ounces fresh cauliflower (cooked in boiling water for one minute and drained) or, 8-ounce package frozen cauliflower florets, thawed

2 teaspoons minced dried onion

1 tablespoon Dijon mustard

¼ cup mayonnaise

¼ cup lowfat sour cream

Salt and pepper to taste

- Place wire rack into bowl of oven. Preheat oven to 500°F.

- Arrange cauliflower in bottom of an 8x8-inch nonstick coated metal baking pan. In a small bowl combine onion, mustard, mayonnaise and sour cream. Season with salt and pepper. Pour sauce over cauliflower. Cover pan with foil.

- Reduce oven heat to 400°F. Bake cauliflower until hot and bubbly, about 10 to 15 minutes.

BROCCOLI, CORN AND PEPPERS WITH LIME BUTTER

Makes 4 Servings

Cooking time: 15 minutes

16-ounce package frozen broccoli, corn and peppers
2 tablespoons butter or margarine, melted
1 teaspoon lime juice
Salt and pepper

- Grease a 9-inch metal baking pan.

- Place wire rack into bowl of oven. Preheat oven to 500°F.

- Arrange vegetables in pan. Drizzle with butter or margarine. Cover pan with foil.

- Reduce oven heat to 400°F. Cook 15 minutes or until tender. Remove from oven. Add lime juice, salt and pepper. Stir.

SWEET AND SOUR BRAISED RED CABBAGE

Makes 6 Servings

Cooking time: 35 to 40 minutes

½ pound bacon, cut into ½-inch pieces

1 cup chopped onions

1½ pounds red cabbage, finely shredded

1 tart apple, peeled, cored and sliced

⅓ cup apple cider

⅓ cup apple cider vinegar

1½ tablespoons brown sugar

½ teaspoon salt

½ teaspoon black pepper

- Place wire rack into bowl of oven. Preheat oven to 500°F.

- Place bacon in a 9-inch metal baking pan.

- Reduce oven heat to 450°F. Cook bacon in oven 15 minutes. Add onions and cook for 10 minutes. Add cabbage, apple, cider, vinegar, sugar, salt and pepper. Cover pan and cook 15 minutes. Check occasionally. Stir and add more cider if too dry.

NEW POTATOES WITH PARSLEY BUTTER

Makes 4 Servings

Cooking time: 15 to 20 minutes

2 teaspoons vegetable oil

2 tablespoons butter or margarine, softened

1 tablespoon fresh chopped parsley

Salt and pepper to taste

12 small new potatoes, peeled and rinsed (you may select any small, thin skin potato)

- Place wire rack into bowl of oven. Preheat oven to 500°F. Coat bottom of 9-inch metal baking pan with 2 teaspoons of oil.

- Prepare parsley butter: In a small bowl blend the softened butter or margarine, parsley, salt and pepper to taste.

- Arrange potatoes in pan. Toss to coat with oil. Reduce oven heat to 450°F. Cook 15 to 20 minutes or until potatoes pierce easily with a fork. Top potatoes with parsley butter and toss to coat.

BABY CARROTS IN LEMON MINT GLAZE

Makes 4 Servings

Cooking time: 20 minutes

2 tablespoons butter or margarine, melted

2 tablespoons sugar

1-pound package baby carrots or 3½ cups carrots cut into ½ x 3-inch pieces

1 tablespoon fresh lemon juice

1½ tablespoons fresh mint, chopped, or 1½ teaspoons dried

- Place wire rack into bowl of oven. Preheat oven to 500°F.

- Coat a 9-inch metal baking pan with the melted butter or margarine. Sprinkle sugar over butter. Add carrots to the pan. Drizzle lemon juice over carrots. Toss and stir to coat carrots.

- Reduce oven heat to 400°F. Bake carrots 15 minutes, stirring every 5 minutes. Add mint. Stir well. Bake another 5 minutes or until tender.

LEMON PEPPER POTATOES

Makes 4 Servings

Cooking time: 15 minutes

1 tablespoon butter or margarine, melted

1 tablespoon vegetable oil

12 small new potatoes cut into 1½-inch chunks

1 teaspoon salt

1 tablespoon lemon pepper seasoning

- Place wire rack into bowl of oven. Preheat oven to 500°F.

- Pour butter and oil into a 9-inch metal baking pan. Add potatoes, salt and lemon-pepper seasoning. Toss all ingredients to coat.

- Reduce oven heat to 400°F. Cook potatoes 15 minutes or until potatoes pierce easily with a fork. Stir and toss every 5 minutes. Be sure to bring unbrowned potatoes up from the bottom so all potatoes brown nicely.

ZIPPY CORN AND RED PEPPER TIMBALES

Makes 4 Servings

Cooking time: 45 minutes to 1 hour

3 eggs

1 cup heavy cream

Dash white wine Worcestershire sauce

½ cup chopped red bell pepper

1 cup corn kernels (if frozen, thaw)

1 tablespoon minced onion

1 teaspoon chili powder

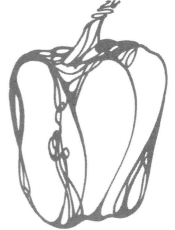

- ■ Grease four 4 or 5-ounce ramekins or souffle dishes.

- ■ Place wire rack into bowl of oven. Preheat oven to 500°F.

- ■ In a bowl, beat together the eggs and heavy cream. Add the Worcestershire sauce, pepper, corn, onion and chili powder. Mix and pour into ramekins.

- ■ Place dishes or ramekins in a 9-inch metal baking pan. Fill pan with water to reach about 1-inch up the sides of the ramekins.

- ■ Reduce oven heat to 350°F. Bake pan 45 minutes to 1 hour or until a knife inserted in the center comes out clean. Let timbales rest in oven 5 minutes. Serve from ramekin or invert to unmold.

BAKED STUFFED POTATOES WITH HERB CHEESE

Makes 4 Servings

Cooking time: 35 to 40 minutes

4 medium baking potatoes, scrubbed

4 teaspoons vegetable oil

8-ounce container herb and garlic cheese spread

¼ cup sour cream

- Place wire rack into bowl of oven. Preheat oven to 500°F.

- Rub each potato with 1 teaspoon of oil.

- Reduce oven heat to 425°F. Bake potatoes directly on wire rack for 30 minutes or until easily pierced with a fork. Remove potatoes and allow to cool slightly.

- Slash skin of potatoes and scoop out pulp. Reserve potato skins. In a small mixer bowl combine potato pulp and cheese spread. Beat with electric mixer until well blended. Add sour cream. Beat until light and fluffy. Stuff filling back into potato skins.

- Return to oven and bake until nicely browned, about 5 minutes.

ROASTED PEPPERS, POTATOES AND GREEN BEANS

Makes 4 Servings

Cooking time: 15 to 20 minutes

Coarsely ground black pepper, ½ teaspoon or to taste
Coarse salt, ½ teaspoon or to taste
2 cups red new potatoes, ½-inch cubes
1¼ cups red bell pepper strips, about 3 x ½-inch
1¼ cups green beans, cut into 2-inch pieces
2 tablespoons olive oil

- Place wire rack into bowl of oven. Preheat oven to 500°F.

- Pour olive oil in a 9-inch metal baking pan. Add potatoes, peppers and beans to pan. Sprinkle with salt and pepper. Toss to mix and coat.

- Reduce oven heat to 400°F. Cook vegetables 15 to 20 minutes or until tender. Turn every 5 minutes.

COOKING VEGETABLES IN A COUNTERTOP CONVECTION OVEN GIVES BETTER RESULTS THAN COOKING THEM IN WATER. WATER TAKES VITAMINS B AND C OUT OF THE VEGETABLES. REMEMBER THIS TIP - THE MORE WATER YOU USE, THE MORE VITAMINS YOU LOSE.

ROASTED BRUSSELS SPROUTS

Cooking time: 20 to 25 minutes

2 tablespoons butter or margarine, melted
2 tablespoons olive oil
1 teaspoon garlic, minced
½ teaspoon salt
1 pound brussels sprouts, washed and trimmed

- Place wire rack into bowl of oven. Preheat oven to 500°F.

- Place butter or margarine, oil, garlic and salt in a 9-inch metal baking pan. Add brussels sprouts. Toss to coat. Cover pan tightly with foil.

- Reduce oven heat to 350°F. Bake sprouts 15 to 20 minutes. Uncover and continue baking 5 minutes until tender.

CAULIFLOWER, BLACK OLIVES AND CAPERS

Makes 2 Servings

Cooking time: 10 to 15 minutes

8-ounces fresh cauliflower (cooked in boiling water for one minute and drained) or, 8-ounce package frozen cauliflower florets, thawed
¼ cup black olives, sliced
2 teaspoons capers, drained
½ teaspoon garlic, minced
1 tablespoon olive oil
Salt and pepper to taste

- Place wire rack into bowl of oven. Preheat oven to 500°F.

- Arrange cauliflower, olives, capers, garlic and oil in an 8-inch metal baking pan. Season with salt and pepper. Toss to coat. Cover pan with foil.

- Reduce oven heat to 400°F. Bake 10 to 15 minutes or until hot.

Roast Beef Melt with
Horseradish Sauce and
Zesty French Fries, *p.166*

Top:
Ham and Cheese
Souffléed Casserole with
Corn Muffins, *p.162*

Left:
Chicken Tandoori Skewers
with Herbed Pitas, *p.159*

Right:
Baked Shells and Cheese with
Sun-Dried Tomatoes and
Fresh Baked Sesame Rolls, *p.160*

Top:
**Tomato, Bacon
and Two Cheese
Strata,** *p.149*

Middle Right:
**Baked Turkey
Sausage and
Eggs with Honey
English Muffins,**
p.139

Bottom:
**Baked Penne
with Fontina and
Pesto,** *p.141*

Top Right:
**Ham and Cheese Sandwich
Italian Style,** *p.144*

Bottom:
**Tuna Melt with Tomatoes
and Capers,** *p.143*

QUICK & COMPLETE MEALS

Quick meals needn't be boring. It's easy to make delicious, healthy and fun foods in your Countertop Convection Oven.

Take **Shrimp Orzo and Artichoke Bake** for instance. It's simply a wonderful way to enjoy cooking and eating with your oven. **Turkey Enchiladas with Spicy Black Beans** is another meal which is anything but ordinary and has incredible taste. For brunch you may want to prepare the **Puffy Pear Pancake** recipe or **Eggs Benedict from the Oven with Quick Hollandaise**. Both will delight the palate of the breakfast and brunch crowd.

Your Countertop Convection Oven is perfect for complete meals. On television I show bacon, sausage and eggs with hash brown potatoes, all cooked at the same time. You can do the same with **Mexican Turkey Burgers with Easy Cheesy Potatoes** or the **Baked Kielbasa with Red Peppers and Carrots.** Many of your family's favorite meal combinations can be created this way.

Remember that different foods require different cooking times just as they do in other appliances. Be sure to note which foods take longer and start them first.

SWEET AND SOUR TURKEY STUFFED CABBAGE ROLLS

Makes 4 Servings

Cooking time: 1 hour and 30 minutes

1 small head cabbage
1 pound ground turkey
¼ cup uncooked rice
2 tablespoons onion, minced
1 teaspoon dried basil
½ teaspoon garlic, minced
1 egg
1½ teaspoons white wine Worcestershire sauce
Salt and pepper to taste

Sauce:
1¼ cups canned chicken broth
¼ cup cider vinegar
¼ cup sugar
2 tablespoons white wine Worcestershire sauce
2 tablespoons cornstarch
Dash of bitters
Cooked rice or noodles

- Grease a 9-inch metal baking pan.
- Bring a large pot of water to a boil. Add cabbage and turn off heat. Allow cabbage to wilt 5 minutes. Remove and drain.
- Place wire rack into bowl of oven. Preheat oven to 500°F.
- Combine ground turkey, rice, onion, basil, garlic, egg, Worcestershire sauce, salt and pepper. Mix well with hands.
- Cut 8 unblemished large leaves from cabbage. Remove center vein from cabbage leaves, keeping each leaf in one piece. Place ⅛ of the filling on each stem end. Roll leaves up, tucking sides in as you go. Tie each roll with kitchen string.
- Arrange rolls seam side down and close together in pan. To make sauce combine broth, vinegar, sugar, Worcestershire sauce, cornstarch and bitters. Pour sauce over rolls. Cover pan with foil.
- Reduce oven heat to 425°F. Bake for about 1 hour and 30 minutes or until tender. Remove string and serve with sauce over rice or noodles.

BAKED TURKEY SAUSAGE AND EGGS WITH HONEY ENGLISH MUFFINS

Makes 4 Servings

Cooking time: 8 to 10 minutes

Sausage and Eggs:
1½ pounds ground turkey
1 teaspoon salt
2 teaspoons fennel seeds, crushed
1 teaspoon coarsely ground black pepper
½ teaspoon dried red pepper flakes, crushed
1 teaspoon garlic, minced
½ teaspoon dry sage (optional)
4 eggs

English Muffins:
4 English muffins, split
4 tablespoons prepared honey butter spread

- Lightly grease wire rack. Place lower wire rack into bowl of oven. Preheat oven to 500°F.

- In a large bowl combine turkey, salt, fennel seeds, pepper, red pepper, garlic and sage (optional). Mix until well blended. Refrigerate 1 hour.

- Shape turkey mixture into 4 patties. Make an indentation in each patty large enough to hold one egg.

- Reduce oven heat to 450°F. Place patties directly on wire rack. Bake patties 3 to 4 minutes. One at a time, break an egg into a glass measuring cup or custard cup and pour carefully into patty. Repeat for all patties. Continue baking until egg is set and cooked, about 5 minutes.

- While eggs are cooking, prepare English muffins. Spread each split muffin with some of the honey butter. Put the upper rack in position over the lower rack. Place the muffin halves, cut and buttered side up, on the rack. Cook until muffins are golden, about 3 minutes.

✔**Check your owner's manual for preheating time which may vary by manufacturer.**

CREAMY RAVIOLI CASSEROLE

Makes 4 to 6 Servings

Cooking time: 40 minutes

2   13-ounce packages frozen round cheese ravioli
(24 to 25, 1½-inch ravioli)

11¼-ounce can condensed Italian-style
tomato soup, undiluted

½ cup canned crushed tomatoes

1 tablespoon fresh chopped basil or 1 teaspoon dried

1 teaspoon garlic, minced

1½ cups half-and-half

2 tablespoons Parmesan cheese

½ cup shredded mozzarella cheese

- Grease an 8x8-inch metal baking pan.

- Place wire rack into bowl of oven. Preheat oven to 500°F.

- Cook ravioli on stovetop according to package directions, reducing cooking time by 5 minutes. Arrange ravioli in pan.

- In a small bowl combine the undiluted soup, tomatoes, basil, garlic and half-and-half. Mix well and pour over ravioli. Top casserole evenly with Parmesan and mozzarella cheeses. Cover pan with foil.

- Reduce oven heat to 425°F. Bake casserole for 30 minutes. Uncover, reduce oven heat to 350°F and continue baking 10 minutes or until casserole is bubbly and cheese is lightly browned. Let casserole rest 5 minutes before serving.

HERE'S A CASSEROLE THAT EVERYONE WHO LOVES ITALIAN FOOD WILL ENJOY. IT INCLUDES TWO OF ITALY'S BEST LOVED CHEESES AND ONE OF ITS POPULAR PASTAS. BON APPÉTIT.

BAKED PENNE WITH FONTINA AND PESTO

Cooking time: 15 minutes

½ cup chopped onion
1 tablespoon olive oil
½ cup ricotta cheese
½ cup heavy cream
½ pound Fontina cheese, grated
½ pound penne, cooked according to package directions
3-ounces pesto sauce

- ■ Grease a 1½ quart casserole.

- ■ In a medium frying pan, saute onion in olive oil until soft. Add ricotta and cream and bring to a boil. Stir in half of the Fontina and cook until it is just melted.

- ■ Place wire rack into bowl of oven. Preheat oven to 500°F.

- ■ Cook pasta and drain. Return to pot. Add cheese and cream mixture and pesto. Toss to coat. Transfer to casserole and top with remaining Fontina cheese. Cover casserole with foil.

- ■ Place a piece of foil the same size as the bottom of the casserole directly on the wire rack. Place casserole on foil.

- ■ Reduce oven heat to 325°F. Bake for 15 minutes or until heated through.

Shrimp Orzo and Artichoke Bake

Makes 4 Servings

Cooking time: 18 to 20 minutes

2 teaspoons vegetable oil
1 pound shrimp, peeled and deveined
7-ounces artichoke hearts, drained
2 cups cooked orzo (rice-shaped pasta)
1 can condensed cream of shrimp soup, undiluted
1 cup half-and-half
½ cup dry white wine
¼ cup chopped pimiento
Salt and pepper to taste

- Place wire rack into bowl of oven. Preheat oven to 500°F.
- Place oil and shrimp in a 9-inch metal baking pan. Toss to coat shrimp and pan.
- Reduce oven heat to 425°F. Cook shrimp 3 to 5 minutes or until they begin to curl. Remove from oven.
- In a medium bowl combine artichokes, orzo, soup, half-and-half, wine and pimiento. Season with salt and pepper. Pour on top of shrimp. Cover pan with foil. Cook at 425°F for 15 minutes until heated through and bubbly.

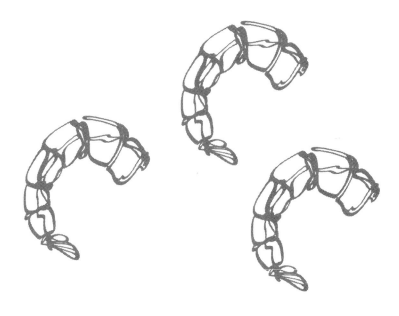

TUNA MELT WITH TOMATOES AND CAPERS

Makes 2 Servings

Cooking time: 4 minutes

6-ounces water packed tuna, drained
¼ cup mayonnaise
1 tablespoon chopped onion
2 teaspoons capers
1 pimiento, drained and chopped
Salt and pepper to taste
2 6-inch long French or Italian Rolls
8 plum tomato slices, cut ¼-inch thick
4-ounces Colby cheese, sliced thin

■ Place wire rack into bowl of oven. Preheat oven to 500°F.

■ In a medium bowl combine the tuna, mayonnaise, onion, capers, pimiento, salt and pepper. Mix well.

■ Slice each roll and open out. Spread each roll with half the tuna mixture. Top each roll with 4 tomato slices then half of the cheese.

■ Keep oven heat at 500°F. Grill sandwiches until cheese melts and filling is heated - about 4 minutes.

WHEN ANY RECIPE CALLS FOR TOMATOES, IT'S BEST TO PREPARE IT WHEN TOMATOES ARE IN SEASON - USUALLY IN LATE SUMMER OR EARLY FALL.

HAM AND CHEESE SANDWICHES ITALIAN STYLE

Makes 2 Servings

Cooking time: 6 minutes

4 slices Italian style white bread
4 teaspoons prepared pesto sauce
4-ounces Fontina cheese, cut into small thin pieces
6 thin slices prosciutto
1 tablespoon olive oil

- Place wire rack into bowl of oven. Preheat oven to 500°F.

- Spread each bread slice with 1 teaspoon pesto. Top 2 bread slices with Fontina pieces,then prosciutto slices and another bread slice. Brush both sides of sandwiches with olive oil.

- Keep oven heat at 500°F. Grill sandwiches 3 minutes. Press down on sandwich with a spatula to compress. Grill another 3 minutes or until golden. Cut each sandwich in half and serve.

EGGS BENEDICT FROM THE OVEN WITH QUICK HOLLANDAISE

Makes 2 Servings

Cooking time: 5 to 6 minutes

1 package Hollandaise sauce mix
4 eggs
4 slices Canadian bacon
2 English muffins, split

- Prepare Hollandaise sauce mix according to package directions and set aside.

- Place lower wire rack into bowl of oven. Preheat oven to 500°F.

- Grease four cups of a 4 or 6-cup muffin tin. Break one egg into each greased muffin cup. Fill unused cups ⅔ full with water. Reduce oven heat to 450°F. Place the tin on the bottom rack. Put the upper rack in place. Cook the eggs for 3 minutes.

- Place Canadian bacon and English muffins, split side up, on upper rack of oven. Continue cooking 3 more minutes or until muffins are toasted and Canadian bacon is hot.

- Gently reheat Hollandaise sauce. Place 2 English muffin halves on each serving plate. Top each with a slice of Canadian bacon, an egg and Hollandaise sauce. Serve immediately.

PUFFED PROVOLONE CUSTARD

Makes 4 Servings

Cooking time: 45 minutes
Refrigerate: Overnight

6 slices Italian style bread, torn up
1½ cups grated or shredded provolone cheese
1½ cups milk
6 eggs, slightly beaten
1 teaspoon seasoned salt

- Grease a 9-inch metal baking pan.

- Distribute the torn bread evenly over the bottom of the pan. Sprinkle cheese over bread. In a small bowl combine milk, eggs and seasoned salt. Pour the mixture over the bread. Cover and refrigerate overnight.

- Place wire rack into bowl of oven. Preheat oven to 500°F.

- Reduce oven heat to 400°F and bake custard for 45 minutes or until puffed and golden.

THIS MAKE-AHEAD TREAT IS PERFECT FOR A SPECIAL WEEKEND BRUNCH. ADD A COLORFUL SALAD OF MIXED GREENS AND FRUIT TO ROUND OUT THE MEAL. THIS IS A WONDERFUL COMBINATION WHEN YOU WANT TO HAVE EVERYTHING PREPARED IN ADVANCE.

EASY CASSOULET

Cooking time: 30 to 35 minutes

2 carrots, peeled and sliced

1 celery stalk, chopped

1 medium onion, chopped

1 tablespoon vegetable oil

2 skinless, boneless chicken breast halves, each cut in 6 pieces

14-ounces pinto beans, drained and rinsed

⅓ pound Kielbasa, cut into ¼-inch diagonal slices

¼ pound cooked ham, cut into ½ inch pieces

1 teaspoon rosemary, crumbled

½ teaspoon thyme

½ cup dry white wine

Salt and pepper

- Grease an 8x8-inch metal baking pan.

- Place wire rack into bowl of oven. Preheat oven to 500°F.

- In a large frying pan, saute the carrots, celery and onion in the vegetable oil until almost tender. Add the chicken pieces and cook until chicken is no longer pink. Transfer mixture to the baking pan. Stir in beans, Kielbasa, ham, rosemary, thyme, wine, salt and pepper. Cover pan with foil.

- Reduce oven heat to 425°F. Bake cassoulet 30 to 35 minutes or until heated through.

GRILLED ITALIAN SAUSAGE WITH RED ONIONS

Cooking time: 12 to 14 minutes

1 tablespoon olive oil

1 tablespoon balsamic vinegar

Salt and pepper to taste

½ pound Italian sausage, cut into 3-inch slices

1 large red onion, peeled and cut lengthwise into eighths

Italian bread

- Place upper rack into bowl of oven. Preheat oven to 500°F.

- Combine oil, vinegar, salt and pepper in a small bowl. Brush mixture on sausage and onions.

- Reduce oven heat to 475°F. Place sausage and onions on upper rack. Cook for 12 to 14 minutes or until onions are nicely browned and sausage is cooked through. Serve on Italian bread.

ROASTED TUNA WITH GRILLED VEGETABLES

Makes 4 Servings

Cooking time: 13 to 15 minutes

1 teaspoon garlic, minced

1 tablespoon balsamic or red wine vinegar

2 tablespoons olive oil

4   6-ounce tuna steaks

1 small zucchini, cut into ½-inch slices

1 small yellow squash, cut into ½-inch slices

1 red bell pepper, cut into ½-inch strips

1 large red onion, cut into quarters and separated

Salt and pepper to taste

- Place lower wire rack into bowl of oven. Preheat oven to 500°F.

- In a small bowl whisk together garlic, vinegar and 1 tablespoon of the oil. Set aside. Brush tuna and vegetables with remaining oil. Sprinkle with salt and liberal amount of pepper.

- Arrange vegetables on wire rack. Reduce oven heat to 450°F. Cook vegetables 5 minutes.

- Place upper wire rack into bowl of oven. Place tuna on upper rack. Cook tuna and vegetables 8 to 10 minutes or until fish flakes easily. Transfer tuna to a serving platter and surround with vegetables. Drizzle vegetables with olive oil, garlic and vinegar mixture. Toss lightly.

OLIVE OIL IS PREFERRED IN MY RECIPES BECAUSE IT ADDS SO MUCH TO THE FLAVOR OF VEGETABLES. ACTUALLY THE VERY BEST OLIVE OILS COME FROM THE TUSCANY REGION OF ITALY. AMERICAN OLIVE OILS DON'T COMPARE.

MEXICAN TURKEY BURGERS WITH EASY CHEESY POTATOES

Makes 4 Servings

Cooking time: 22 to 23 minutes

Burgers:

1¼ pound ground turkey

1 tablespoon dried minced onion

2 teaspoons chili powder

1 teaspoon ground cumin

1 teaspoon lime juice

Salt and pepper to taste

Potatoes:

1-pound can peeled white potatoes, drained and sliced

½ of an 11-ounce can Cheddar cheese soup

¾ cup half-and-half or milk

¾ cup shredded Monterey Jack cheese

■ Grease an 8 or 9-inch metal baking pan.

■ Place wire rack into bowl of oven. Preheat oven to 500°F. Lightly oil upper rack, set aside.

■ In a medium bowl combine turkey, onion, chili powder, cumin, lime juice, salt and pepper. Mix well and shape into four 3½ to 4-inch patties. Refrigerate until needed.

■ In baking pan, combine potatoes, soup and half-and-half. Top with cheese. Cover pan with foil.

■ Reduce oven heat to 425°F. Bake potatoes 15 minutes.

■ Put upper wire rack into position over potatoes. Place turkey burgers directly on wire rack. Increase oven heat to 475°F and grill burgers 7 to 8 minutes or until desired degree of doneness. Serve burgers with potatoes.

UNTIL RECENTLY THE POPULARITY OF GROUND BEEF HAS NEVER BEEN CHALLENGED. USED IN A VARIETY OF RECIPES SUCH AS HAMBURGERS AND MEAT LOAF, BEEF RULED THE ROOST. TODAY, GROUND TURKEY AND CHICKEN HAVE ENTERED THE RACE AND HAVE WON A STRONG FOLLOWING AMONG HEALTH-CONSCIOUS AMERICANS.

Tomato, Bacon and Two Cheese Strata

Makes 4 to 6 Servings

Cooking time: 55 to 60 minutes

2 cups white bread, torn into small pieces
½ cup sharp Cheddar cheese, grated
½ cup mild Cheddar cheese, grated
4 slices bacon, cooked until crisp, drained and crumbled
3 Italian plum tomatoes, sliced into ¼-inch slices
½ cup milk
3 eggs, slightly beaten
½ teaspoon black pepper

- Place wire rack into bowl of oven. Preheat oven to 500°F.

- Grease an 8 or 9-inch metal baking pan.

- Arrange torn bread in bottom of pan. Combine the cheeses. Sprinkle bread with ½ the cheese, all the bacon and tomato slices. Sprinkle with remaining cheese.

- Beat together the milk, eggs and pepper. Pour over the ingredients in pan. Cover pan tightly with foil and seal around edges to secure.

- Reduce oven heat to 400°F. Bake 55 to 60 minutes or until set and lightly browned.

CHEDDAR IS AN ALL-AMERICAN CHEESE. IT IS AVAILABLE FROM MILD TO VERY SHARP. THE ABOVE RECIPE USES TWO VARIETIES. YOU'LL FIND THIS VERY FIRM TO CRUMBLY CHEESE IS POPULAR NOT ONLY IN RECIPES BUT ALSO AS A SNACK SERVED WITH CRACKERS AND FRUIT. AT OUR HOUSE, WE USE CHEDDAR IN SAUCES, SANDWICHES AND SALADS, IN ADDITION TO BREADS AND MAIN DISHES.

GIANT ORANGE SCENTED BACON POPOVER

Makes 4 Servings

Cooking time: 25 minutes

2 eggs, lightly beaten
1 cup milk
1 tablespoon vegetable oil
1 cup all-purpose flour
Grated rind of 1 large orange
Pinch salt
½ pound bacon, cooked, drained and broken into 1-inch pieces

- Grease bottom and 1 inch up the sides of a 9-inch metal baking pan.

- Place wire rack into bowl of oven. Preheat oven to 500°F.

- In a medium bowl combine eggs, milk and oil. Stir in flour, rind and salt. Beat with an electric mixer at medium speed until smooth - about 30 seconds. Pour batter into pan and arrange bacon pieces in batter.

- Reduce oven heat to 400°F. Bake popover 15 minutes. Remove from oven. Lift edge of popover with a fork and flip it over in the pan so that the bottom is now on top.

- Return popover to oven and bake 8 to 10 more minutes. Inside of popover will be very moist. Serve with a fruit flavored syrup.

IF YOU LIKE POPOVERS, TRY THIS RECIPE. AFTER A RECENT TV DEMONSTRATION, WE HAD THE ENTIRE STAGE CREW BEGGING FOR THE RECIPE. WHEN YOU MAKE IT FOR GUESTS, YOU'LL PROBABLY GET THE SAME REACTION.

Puffy Pear Pancake

Makes 2 Servings

Cooking time: 12 to 14 minutes

1 tablespoon butter or margarine, melted

4 canned pear halves, well drained and diced

5 tablespoons sugar

1 teaspoon grated lemon peel

⅛ teaspoon nutmeg

3 eggs, at room temperature

6 tablespoons milk

⅓ cup all-purpose flour

½ teaspoon vanilla

Pinch salt

¼ teaspoon baking powder

2 tablespoons butter or margarine, melted

1 tablespoon sugar mixed with ¼ teaspoon nutmeg and ⅛ teaspoon cinnamon

- Pour one tablespoon melted butter or margarine in a 9-inch metal baking pan.

- Place wire rack into bowl of oven. Preheat oven to 500°F.

- Mix pears, 1 tablespoon sugar, lemon peel and nutmeg in a small bowl. Beat eggs in a medium bowl until light and fluffy. Add remaining sugar, 1 tablespoon at a time to eggs.

- Stir together in a separate bowl the milk, flour, vanilla, salt and baking powder until smooth. Gently fold the milk mixture into the eggs, then fold in the pears. Pour the batter into pan.

- Reduce oven heat to 400°F. Bake the pancake until puffed and springy, about 12 minutes. Brush with melted butter or margarine and sprinkle with sugar mixture. Bake 1 more minute. Cut into wedges and serve immediately.

SHRIMP AND FONTINA PIZZA

Makes 2 to 4 Servings

Cooking time: 5 to 6 minutes

½ pound small or medium shrimp, cooked, shelled, deveined and split in half lengthwise

2 teaspoons olive oil

½ teaspoon garlic, minced

2 small prebaked pizza crust

½ pound shredded Fontina cheese

½ teaspoon dried oregano

Salt and pepper

- Place wire rack into bowl of oven. Preheat oven to 500°F.

- Combine shrimp, oil and garlic in a small bowl. Toss to coat shrimp.

- Arrange half the shrimp on each crust. Top each with half the cheese. Sprinkle with oregano. Season with salt and pepper if desired. Cut each pizza into 4 wedges.

- Reduce oven heat to 425°F. Arrange wedges on upper rack. Cook 5 to 6 minutes until heated through and cheese is melted.

SHRIMP AND FONTINA PIZZA CAN BE MADE ON ANY PIZZA DOUGH RECIPE OR PREBAKED PIZZA SHELLS. THIS MEDITERRANEAN-INSPIRED RECIPE WILL BE A HIT WITH GUESTS.

TURKEY ENCHILADAS WITH SPICY BLACK BEANS

Makes 2 Servings

Cooking time: 25 to 30 minutes

Enchiladas:
2 tablespoons dry minced onion
1 teaspoon garlic, minced
5-ounces frozen spinach, thawed and squeezed dry
1½ cups lowfat sour cream
1 cup cooked turkey, chopped
4-ounces chopped green chilies
1 tablespoon jalapeno peppers, chopped
1 teaspoon chili powder
½ teaspoon ground cumin
4   7½-inch flour tortillas
¾ cups shredded Monterey Jack cheese

Beans:
1 cup canned black beans, rinsed
½ cup medium, hot or mild prepared salsa

■ Grease an 8x8-inch metal baking dish.

■ Place lower wire rack into bowl of oven. Preheat oven to 500°F.

■ In a small bowl combine the onion, garlic, spinach and sour cream. Mix until well blended. Divide mixture in half, placing one half into another bowl. Reserve one bowl. To other bowl add chopped turkey, chilies, jalapenos, chili powder and cumin.

■ Lay tortillas on a work surface. Spread each with some of the turkey mixture. Roll up and place seam side down in baking dish. Pour reserved sour cream mixture over enchiladas and top with shredded cheese.

■ Reduce oven heat to 350°F. Bake enchiladas 15 to 20 minutes until heated through and cheese is melted. Cover with foil if browning too quickly.

■ While enchiladas bake, combine the beans and salsa in a small saucepan and heat on stove top until hot. Serve on top of enchiladas. When the enchiladas have baked 15 minutes place the upper rack in position over the bottom rack. Top the bowl with the extender ring. Place a square of foil the same size as the baking dish on the rack, top it with baking dish of beans. Bake beans along with enchiladas 10 minutes or until beans are hot and enchiladas are heated and cheese is melted.

FENNEL BAKED COD WITH TOMATOES AND FETA CHEESE

Cooking time: 20 minutes

Cod:
24-ounces cod, cut into four 6-ounce pieces
2 tablespoons fresh lemon juice
2 tablespoons olive oil
1 fennel bulb, cut into slices ¼-inch wide
1 teaspoon fennel seeds
Salt and pepper to taste
1 lemon, sliced thin

Tomatoes:
28-ounce can whole Italian plum tomatoes
½ cup crumbled feta cheese
2 tablespoons chopped red onion
Pepper to taste

■ Grease a 9-inch metal baking pan.

■ Place lower wire rack into bowl of oven. Preheat oven to 500°F.

■ Place the cod pieces in pan. Sprinkle with lemon juice, olive oil, fennel slices, fennel seeds, salt, pepper and lemon slices. Cover pan with foil.

■ Reduce oven heat to 425°F. Bake fish 15 minutes or until it flakes easily with a fork.

■ While fish cooks, prepare tomatoes. Carefully slice tomatoes into ¼-inch slices. Arrange them in a small glass or ceramic baking dish. Sprinkle with feta cheese, onion and pepper.

■ When fish has cooked 12 minutes put upper rack in place. Place a square of aluminum foil the same size as the bottom of the baking dish directly on the upper rack. Place the dish with tomatoes on the foil and bake 7 minutes or until tomatoes are hot and feta is browned.

■ Place cod on serving platter and surround with tomatoes.

WESTERN BEAN BAKE AND HOT ROLLS

Makes 4 Servings

Cooking time: 40 minutes

16-ounce can pork and beans

8-ounces canned black beans, drained and rinsed

2 tablespoons dry minced onion

¼ cup catsup

1 tablespoon molasses

1 tablespoon brown sugar

1 teaspoon Dijon mustard

½ teaspoon bitters

2 teaspoons cider vinegar

1 4-ounce Kielbasa, cut into ⅜ inch slices

2 2-ounce hot dogs, cut into ⅜ inch slices

1 can ready to bake rolls

■ Grease an 8-inch round metal baking pan.

■ Place lower wire rack into bowl of oven. Preheat oven to 500°F.

■ In a bowl combine pork and beans, black beans, onion, catsup, molasses, brown sugar, mustard, bitters and vinegar. Stir to combine. Arrange Kielbasa and hot dogs in bottom of pan and pour bean mixture over them. Cover pan with foil.

■ Reduce oven heat to 350°F. Bake beans 15 minutes or until heated through.

■ After 15 minutes put upper rack in place and top bowl with extender ring. Arrange rolls on upper rack. Keep oven heat to 350°F. Bake rolls and beans 25 minutes. Serve everything hot.

WESTERN STYLE NEVER TASTED SO GOOD. WITH THIS UNIQUE COMBINATION OF PORK AND BEANS AND BLACK BEANS MIXED WITH KIELBASA AND HOT DOGS, YOU'LL DELIGHT EVERYONE IN THE BUNK HOUSE.

TORTELLINI BROCCOLI BAKE WITH HERB GARLIC TOAST

Makes 4 Servings

Cooking time: 20 minutes

Tortellini:

7-ounce package tricolor cheese tortellini

½ cup chopped onion

1 teaspoon olive oil

¾ cups ricotta cheese

⅓ cup prepared Caesar dressing

10-ounce package frozen broccoli, thawed

Salt and pepper to taste

½ cup Parmesan cheese, grated

Toast:

½ of 1 pound loaf of Italian bread

4 tablespoons butter or margarine, softened

1 teaspoon chopped garlic

1 teaspoon Italian seasoning

- Grease an 8x8-inch metal baking dish.

- Place lower wire rack into bowl of oven. Preheat oven to 500°F.

- Cook tortellini according to package directions and drain. Reserve ½ cup cooking liquid.

- In a medium frying pan, saute onion in 1 teaspoon olive oil until tender.

- Arrange tortellini in bottom of baking pan. In a bowl combine onion, ricotta, dressing, broccoli, reserved cooking liquid, salt and pepper. Pour over tortellini. Stir gently to coat. Top with grated Parmesan. Cover pan with foil.

- Reduce oven heat to 400°F. Bake tortellini 20 minutes or until heated through.

- Cut the bread into 8 slices. Blend the butter or margarine, garlic and Italian seasoning in a small bowl. Spread each piece of bread with some of the mixture.

- Place upper rack in position over bottom rack holding tortellini. Increase oven heat to 475°F. Place bread slices on upper rack and cook for 1 to 2 minutes or until brown.

FONTINA AND PROSCIUTTO LASAGNA WITH HOT POPPY SEED BREAD

Makes 4 Servings

Cooking time: 30 to 35 minutes

Lasagna:

1 small onion, chopped

2 teaspoons olive oil

14-ounces crushed tomatoes

2 teaspoons dried rosemary, crushed

Pinch dried red pepper flakes

Salt and pepper to taste

15-ounces ricotta cheese

1 egg

6 lasagna noodles cut to fit an 8x8 inch metal baking pan, cooked and drained

1 cup shredded Fontina cheese (about ½ pound)

⅔ cups grated Parmesan cheese

1 small bunch escarole, rinsed, chopped and cooked in boiling water 7 minutes and drained.

½ cup chopped prosciutto (about 2 ounces)

Bread:

1 can ready to bake bread

1 egg, beaten

1 tablespoon poppy seeds

- Grease an 8x8-inch metal baking pan and upper rack of oven.
- Place lower wire rack into bowl of oven. Preheat oven to 500°F.
- In a saucepan saute the onion until soft in 2 teaspoons oil. Add crushed tomatoes, rosemary, red pepper flakes, salt and pepper. Simmer five minutes.
- In a bowl blend the ricotta and egg. Mix well.
- Spread a little of the sauce in the bottom of the baking pan and top with a layer of noodles. Top noodles with ½ of the ricotta/egg mixture, ⅓ of the Fontina, ⅓ of the Parmesan, ½ of the escarole and ½ of the prosciutto. Spoon on more sauce. Make another layer of noodles and repeat other ingredients in the same amounts. Top with a final layer of noodles. Top with the remainder of the sauce, Fontina and Parmesan. Cover pan with foil.
- Reduce oven heat to 350°F. Bake lasagna 5 minutes.
- While lasagna bakes, prepare bread. Open can of bread and place on a floured surface. Bring ends of loaf together to form a ring. Press ends together to seal. Brush bread with beaten egg. Sprinkle with seeds. After lasagna has baked 5 minutes, place greased upper rack in position over lower rack holding lasagna. Place bread directly on upper rack. Bake lasagna and bread together for 30 minutes or until lasagna is heated through and bread is golden brown. Serve lasagna and bread together with tossed salad.

SMOKED HONEY MUSTARD PORK CHOPS WITH BAKED SWEET POTATO ROUNDS

Makes 2 Servings

Cooking time: 16 to 18 minutes

Sweet Potatoes:

2 medium sweet potatoes or yams, peeled and sliced into ½ inch rounds

1 tablespoon butter or margarine, melted

¼ teaspoon ground ginger

Pinch salt

Pork Chops:

4 2-ounce boneless smoked pork chops

2 tablespoons honey

1 tablespoon grainy mustard

- Place lower wire rack into bowl of oven. Preheat oven to 500°F.

- Place sweet potatoes, butter or margarine, ginger and salt in an 8 or 9-inch metal baking pan. Toss to coat potatoes.

- Reduce oven heat to 400°F. Bake potatoes 12 minutes.

- While potatoes cook, prepare chops. In a small bowl, blend the honey and mustard. Coat each chop with mixture.

- When potatoes have cooked 12 minutes, put upper rack in position over bottom rack. Increase oven heat to 450°F. Place chops directly on upper rack and cook until hot and browned, about 4 to 6 minutes. Potatoes are done when tender.

- Arrange and serve together.

CHICKEN TANDOORI SKEWERS WITH HERBED PITAS

Makes 4 Servings

Cooking time: 16 to 19 minutes
Marinate: 3 hours or overnight

1 cup plain yogurt

2 tablespoons lime juice

1½ teaspoons ground ginger

2 teaspoons garlic, minced

2 teaspoons paprika

1 teaspoon chili powder

2 teaspoons ground cumin

1 teaspoon coriander

1 teaspoon hot sauce

1 pound boneless, skinless chicken breasts, cut into 1-inch cubes

1 pound broccoli

16 cherry tomatoes

1 pita bread, split in half lengthwise

1 tablespoon melted butter or margarine

½ teaspoon oregano

■ Combine the yogurt, lime juice, ginger, garlic, paprika, chili powder, cumin, coriander and hot sauce in a medium bowl. Add the chicken and toss to coat. Refrigerate 3 hours or overnight.

■ Place lower wire rack into bowl of oven. Preheat oven to 500°F.

■ Cut broccoli into florets. Cook 2 minutes in boiling water, then drain and rinse in cold water. Thread equal amounts of chicken, broccoli and cherry tomatoes on each skewer.

■ Reduce oven heat to 450°F. Place skewers directly on wire rack. Cook chicken skewers 14 minutes. While chicken cooks, prepare pita bread. Brush each pita half with melted butter or margarine and sprinkle with oregano. Cut each half into 4 wedges.

■ After chicken has cooked 14 minutes, put upper rack in position. Place pita wedges on upper rack and cook 2 to 3 minutes or until just brown. Serve skewers with pita bread.

BAKED SHELLS AND CHEESE WITH SUN-DRIED TOMATOES AND FRESH-BAKED SESAME ROLLS

Makes 4 Servings

Cooking time: 15 to 20 minutes

2 cups shell pasta, cooked and drained
¾ cup shredded mozzarella cheese
½ cup ricotta cheese
⅓ cup oil-packed, sun-dried tomatoes, drained and chopped
½ cup milk
½ teaspoon red pepper flakes
Salt and pepper to taste

Fresh-Baked Sesame Rolls:
11–ounce can ready-to-bake bread
1 egg, beaten with 1 tablespoon water
2 tablespoons sesame seeds

- Grease an 8-inch round metal baking pan.

- Place wire rack into bowl of oven. Preheat oven to 500°F.

- Spread cooked pasta in bottom of pan. Sprinkle with mozzarella. Spoon on ricotta and sun-dried tomatoes. Pour milk over all ingredients. Season with pepper flakes, salt and pepper.

- Reduce oven heat to 350°F. Bake shells 5 minutes. Stir ingredients to combine well and cover pan with foil.

- While shells cook, place bread dough loaf on a floured surface. Cut the loaf to make 8 rolls. Brush the tops of each roll with beaten egg and sprinkle with sesame seeds.

- When shells have cooked 5 minutes, put greased upper rack into position over lower rack with shells. Place sesame rolls on upper rack. Add extender ring. Bake everything 15 minutes or until shells are hot and rolls are golden brown.

SAVORY HAM PATTIES AND BABY CORN WITH CHILI BUTTER

Makes 4 Servings

Cooking time: 17 to 20 minutes

Ham:
1 pound ham, ground
1 tablespoon finely chopped onion
1 tablespoon pickle relish
¼ cup finely chopped celery
¼ cup mayonnaise
¼ cup light sour cream
1 cup dry bread crumbs

Corn:
16-ounce can baby corn
1 to 2 tablespoons butter or margarine
1 teaspoon finely minced jalapeno peppers
1 tablespoon chopped canned green chilies
Salt and pepper to taste

■ Grease a 9-inch round metal baking pan.

■ Place lower wire rack into bowl of oven. Preheat oven to 500°F.

■ In a bowl combine the ham, onion, relish, celery, mayonnaise, sour cream and ¼ cup of the bread crumbs. Mix well and form into 4 patties.

■ Spread remaining crumbs on a plate. Coat the patties with crumbs. Arrange patties in pan. Reduce oven heat to 425°F. Bake patties 10 minutes.

■ While patties bake, prepare corn. Place corn in a small glass or ceramic baking dish. Combine butter or margarine, peppers and chilies in a small saucepan. Cook over low heat until butter melts. Pour chili butter over corn and toss to coat. Season with salt and pepper.

■ When patties have cooked 10 minutes, put upper rack in position in oven. Top bowl with extender ring. Place a square of foil the same size as baking dish on the upper rack. Place baking dish on foil square. Cook corn along with patties 7 to 10 minutes until heated through.

HAM AND CHEESE SOUFFLÉED CASSEROLE WITH CORN MUFFINS

Makes 4 Servings

Cooking time: 30 to 35 minutes

4 eggs
⅓ cup flour
¾ teaspoon baking powder
¾ cup milk
⅔ cup cottage cheese
2-ounces cream cheese, cut into bits
¾ pound Monterey Jack cheese, cut into ½-inch cubes
½ cup finely shredded smoked ham
1 tablespoon fresh parsley, chopped
1 tablespoon onion, minced
Pepper to taste

Corn Muffin:
1-ounce package corn muffin mix

- Grease an 8x8-inch metal baking pan.

- Place wire rack into bowl of oven. Preheat oven to 500°F.

- In a large bowl beat eggs. Stir in flour and baking powder, then milk. Stir in cottage cheese, cream cheese, Monterey Jack cheese, ham, parsley, onion and pepper. Pour into pan.

- Reduce oven heat to 400°F. Bake 20 minutes.

- While casserole bakes, prepare muffin mix as directed. Pour into a greased 6-cup muffin tin. When muffins have baked 20 minutes, put upper rack in position over lower rack. Top bowl with extender ring. Place muffin tin on upper rack. Bake muffins, along with casserole, 10 to 15 minutes or until muffins are brown and casserole is puffed and brown.

MINI MEAT LOAVES WITH QUICK ZUCCHINI PARMESAN

Makes 4 Servings

Cooking time: 25 minutes

Meat Loaf:
1 pound meat loaf mixture or ground beef
1 small onion, chopped
½ cup soft bread crumbs
1 egg, slightly beaten
1 tablespoon fresh basil or ½ teaspoon dried
½ teaspoon dried thyme
½ teaspoon garlic, minced
1 tablespoon Worcestershire sauce
Salt and pepper to taste

Zucchini:
16-ounce can zucchini in Italian tomato sauce
7-ounce jar pimientos, chopped
⅓ cup Parmesan cheese
⅓ cup mild Cheddar or Mozzarella cheese, shredded

- ■ Lightly grease lower wire rack. Place wire rack into bowl of oven. Preheat oven to 500°F.

- ■ In a large bowl combine the meat, onion, bread crumbs, egg, basil, thyme, garlic, Worcestershire sauce, salt and pepper. Mix well with hands and shape into four small loaves.

- ■ Reduce oven heat to 400°F. Place loaves directly on lower rack and bake 15 minutes.

- ■ While loaves are cooking, prepare zucchini. Pour zucchini with tomato sauce into an ungreased 8x8-inch nonstick coated metal baking pan. Stir in chopped pimientos. Top with cheeses in an even layer. Top bowl with extender ring. Bake zucchini along with loaves 10 minutes or until zucchini is heated through and cheese is melted and lightly browned.

BLT Pizza

Cooking time: 5 minutes

6 slices bacon, crisply cooked, drained and broken into ½-inch pieces

4 plum tomatoes, sliced in ¼-inch rounds

1½ cups shredded lettuce

¼ cup salad dressing or mayonnaise

2 small prebaked pizza crusts

Shredded lettuce for garnish

- Place upper rack into bowl of oven. Preheat oven to 500°F.

- In a medium bowl combine bacon, tomatoes, shredded lettuce and salad dressing. Mix gently. Spread ½ of the mixture on each pizza crust. Cut each pizza into 4 wedges.

- Reduce oven heat to 425°F. Arrange pizza crust on upper rack. Cook until heated through - about 5 minutes. Garnish with shredded lettuce.

THE ALL-AMERICAN BLT NEVER TASTED SO GOOD. WHEN COMBINED WITH AN ITALIAN PIZZA SHELL IT BECOMES A WHOLE NEW INTERNATIONAL FAVORITE. IT'S FUN TO PUT A NEW TWIST ON AN OLD FAVORITE.

Fajita Filets with Tex-Mex Macaroni Medley

Cooking time: 10 to 12 minutes
Marinate: 30 minutes

Fajita Filets:
4   1-inch thick filet mignon
2 tablespoons lime juice
2 tablespoons orange juice
1 teaspoon garlic, minced
1 tablespoon vegetable oil
Salt and pepper to taste

Tex-Mex Macaroni Medley:
½ cup elbow macaroni, cooked and drained
½ cup frozen peas, thawed
½ cup frozen corn, thawed
1 cup crushed tomatoes
½ teaspoon ground cumin
2 teaspoons chili powder
1 teaspoon oregano
Salt and pepper to taste
½ cup crushed tortilla chips
¼ cup grated Monterey Jack cheese

- On a flat work surface, lightly pound filet between 2 sheets of plastic wrap, until ½-inch thick.

- In a 9x13-inch glass baking dish, combine lime juice, orange juice, garlic, oil, salt and pepper. Add meat and toss to coat. Cover and refrigerate for 30 minutes.

- Place wire rack into bowl of oven. Preheat oven to 500°F.

- In an 8-inch round greased metal baking dish, combine the macaroni, peas, corn, crushed tomatoes, cumin, chili powder, oregano, salt and pepper. Stir to combine well. Top with crushed tortilla chips and cheese.

- Reduce oven heat to 400°F. Bake macaroni medley 5 to 6 minutes on lower rack. Put upper rack in place over lower rack. Increase oven heat to 475°F. Broil filet on upper rack 4 to 6 minutes or until desired degree of doneness. Serve filet and medley with guacamole and sour cream if desired.

ROAST BEEF MELT WITH HORSERADISH SAUCE AND ZESTY FRENCH FRIES

Makes 2 Servings

Cooking time: 13 to 15 minutes

¼ cup mayonnaise

1 tablespoon prepared horseradish

1 teaspoon Dijon mustard

2 Kaiser rolls, split

½ pound thinly sliced deli roast beef

¼ pound thinly sliced swiss cheese

½ pound frozen french fries

2 teaspoons vegetable oil

1 tablespoon Cajun seasoning

■ Place lower wire rack into bowl of oven. Preheat oven to 500°F. Cover upper rack with foil.

■ In a small bowl blend mayonnaise, horseradish and mustard. Open rolls and spread both sides with horseradish sauce. Place half the roast beef and half the swiss cheese in each roll. Close sandwiches. Lay out two 12x12-inch sheets of foil. Place one sandwich in the center of each foil square. Wrap foil around sandwich to form a neat package.

■ Reduce oven heat to 425°F. Bake sandwiches 5 minutes.

■ Meanwhile, in a 9-inch metal baking pan, toss french fries with oil. Sprinkle evenly with cajun seasoning. Put upper rack in place. Place pan on rack and increase oven heat to 475°F. Bake potatoes until crisp and golden, 8 to 10 minutes, stirring several times during cooking. Bake sandwiches until heated through and cheese is melted.

BAKED CHILIES RELLENOS

Makes 4 Servings

Cooking time: 20 minutes

8-ounces whole green chilies

2 cups shredded Monterey Jack cheese

2 large eggs

1 cup milk

½ cup yellow cornmeal

½ cup buttermilk baking mix (such as Bisquick)

½ teaspoon baking powder

Pinch salt

- Place wire rack into bowl of oven. Preheat oven to 500°F

- Grease an 8x8-inch metal baking pan. Open the chilies and lay flat in the bottom of the baking pan. Spread cheese evenly over layer of chilies.

- In a medium bowl whisk together the eggs and milk. In another bowl, blend well the cornmeal, baking mix, baking powder and salt. Add the eggs and milk, mixing well with whisk or electric mixer. Pour batter over cheese and chilies.

- Reduce oven heat to 450°F. Bake 20 minutes. Serve with salsa.

HOT CORNED BEEF SPECIAL POCKETS WITH GERMAN POTATO SALAD

Makes 4 Servings

Cooking time: 10 minutes

12-ounces of thinly sliced corned beef, torn into bite sized pieces
1 cup prepared cole slaw
2 tablespoons grainy mustard
2 whole wheat pita breads (about 6-inches in diameter), cut in half
3 cups German potato salad or 1½ pounds

- Place wire rack into bowl of oven. Preheat oven at 500°F.

- Spread the inside of the pita halves with mustard. Fill each half with 3 ounces corned beef and ¼ cup cole slaw.

- Lay out four 9x12-inch sheets of foil. Place a filled pita half in center of each foil sheet. Fold foil around each pita to form a neat package.

- Reduce oven heat to 400°F. Bake pitas 5 minutes on lower rack. Place upper rack into position. Top bowl with extender ring.

- When pitas have baked for 5 minutes, place potato salad in an 8x8-inch metal baking pan on upper rack. Bake potato salad until hot and bubbly, about 5 minutes. Serve pitas and salad immediately.

BAKED KIELBASA WITH RED PEPPERS AND CARROTS

Makes 2 Servings

Cooking time: 15 to 20 minutes

2 teaspoons butter or margarine
1 teaspoon vegetable oil
1 large red pepper, seeded and cut into 1-inch strips
2 large carrots, peeled and sliced into ¼-inch rounds
Salt to taste
1 teaspoon (or to taste) lemon pepper seasoning
½ pound Kielbasa cut into 3-inch pieces

- Place wire rack into bowl of oven. Preheat oven to 500°F.

- Place butter or margarine and vegetable oil into a 9-inch metal baking pan. Reduce oven heat to 425°F. Place pan in oven. Cook until butter melts.

- Add vegetables to pan and season with salt and lemon pepper. Stir to coat with seasonings. Cook 15 minutes. Add Kielbasa and cook 5 minutes or until Kielbasa is nicely browned and hot.

Winter Plum
Cobbler, *p.180*

Top Left:
Chocolate Pecan Tarts, *p.185*

Top Right:
Julie's Chocolate Alligator Cookies, *p.187*

Bottom:
Beth's Quick Lemon Almond Pound Cake, *p.190*

Top:
*Pear and Cranberry
Crumble, p.190*

Bottom:
*Applesauce Cake with
Orange Glaze, p.175*

Top Left:
Ruth Ellen's Cinnamon Sugar Cookies, *p.179*

Top Right:
Mint Topped Brownies, *p.178*

Bottom:
Saucy Lemon Cake Cups, *p.174*

DESSERTS

My favorite part of the meal is dessert.

In this section you have an assortment of my very best-loved treats - like **Maine Blueberry Cake with Blueberry Sauce** - that are favorites at the Warden household. How about **Applesauce Cake with Orange Glaze**? And I can't forget **Jeremy's Fudge Brownie Pudding Cups**. I've already eaten too many of those.

Quick Peach and Raspberry Cobbler is so delicious that you'll want to try it after any meal. During the colder months, you'll want to make the **Winter Plum Cobbler** as a festive treat before, during and after the holidays.

Speaking of holidays, don't miss the **Holiday Mincemeat Squares with Lemon Glaze**. They will become an annual holiday favorite, especially around Thanksgiving and Christmas.

Actually, dessert time is anytime with your Countertop Convection Oven, because it's so quick and easy to bake with.

Jeremy's Fudge Brownie Pudding Cups

Makes 4

Cooking time: 10 minutes

½ cup all-purpose flour

¼ cup sugar

3 tablespoons unsweetened cocoa powder

1 teaspoon baking powder

¼ cup evaporated milk

1 tablespoon butter or margarine, melted

⅓ cup sugar

¾ cup boiling water

Ice cream

- Grease four 5-ounce custard cups or souffle dishes.

- Place wire rack into bowl of oven. Preheat oven to 500°F.

- Combine flour, ¼ cup sugar, 1 tablespoon of the cocoa powder and baking powder in a small bowl. Add milk and butter or margarine. Stir until smooth. Spoon batter evenly into custard cups. Combine ⅓ cup sugar and remaining cocoa powder. Gradually stir into boiling water. Pour equal amounts into each custard cup over batter.

- Reduce oven heat to 350°F and bake cups for 10 minutes. Allow to cool 20 minutes. Serve warm or at room temperature with ice cream.

Saucy Lemon Cake Cups

Makes 4

Cooking time: 15 minutes

¼ cup buttermilk baking mix (such as Bisquick)

1 teaspoon grated lemon rind

3 tablespoons fresh lemon juice

2 tablespoons butter or margarine, melted

1 cup milk

2 eggs

⅓ cup sugar

- Grease four 5-ounce custard cups or souffle dishes.

- Place wire rack into bowl of oven. Preheat oven to 500°F.

- In a small bowl combine baking mix and lemon rind. Add juice, butter or margarine and milk. In a medium bowl beat eggs with sugar until light and fluffy. Fold egg mixture into lemon batter. Pour evenly into custard cups.

- Reduce oven heat to 350°F. Place custard cups in a 9-inch metal baking pan. Place pan and cups in oven. Pour 1-inch boiling water into pan. Bake for 15 minutes or until golden and puffed.

APPLESAUCE CAKE WITH ORANGE GLAZE

Makes 1 Cake

Cooking time: 45 minutes

2 cups all-purpose flour
1 cup sugar
½ teaspoon salt
1 teaspoon cinnamon
½ teaspoon nutmeg
¼ teaspoon cloves
1 teaspoon baking soda
2 teaspoons baking powder
1 cup raisins
½ cup melted butter or margarine
2 cups apple sauce

Glaze:
1cup powdered sugar
1 tablespoon melted butter or margarine
2 tablespoons orange juice

- Grease 9-inch metal square or round baking pan.

- Place wire rack into bowl of oven. Preheat oven to 500°F.

- In a large bowl combine the flour, sugar, salt, cinnamon, nutmeg, cloves, baking soda and baking powder. Stir in raisins, butter or margarine and applesauce.

- Reduce oven heat to 350°F. Pour batter into pan and bake for 20 minutes. Remove from oven. Cover tightly with foil. Return to oven and continue baking for 25 minutes or until cake tester inserted in center comes out clean. Cool on wire rack.

- To make glaze: In a small bowl combine powdered sugar, melted butter and orange juice. Mix with a whisk until smooth. Drizzle over cooled cake.

SOUR CREAM GINGERBREAD

Cooking time: 35 minutes

1½ cups all-purpose flour	1 cup dark brown sugar, firmly packed
½ teaspoon salt	
1 teaspoon baking soda	⅓ cup vegetable oil
½ teaspoon cinnamon	1 egg
1 teaspoon ground ginger	1 cup sour cream
¼ teaspoon nutmeg	Whipped cream or lemon sauce

- ■ Grease an 8x8-inch metal baking pan.

- ■ Place wire rack into bowl of oven. Preheat oven to 500°F.

- ■ In a small bowl combine the flour, salt, baking soda, cinnamon, ginger and nutmeg. In a large mixer bowl use an electric mixer to beat the brown sugar, oil and egg. When well combined, add the flour mixture alternately with the sour cream, beginning and ending with the flour mixture. Pour batter into pan.

- ■ Reduce oven heat to 350°F. Bake gingerbread 35 minutes or until cake tester inserted in the middle comes out clean. Cool in pan 10 minutes. Turn out of pan and cool on wire rack. Serve with whipped cream or lemon sauce.

THREE BERRY CRUMBLE

Makes 4 Servings

Cooking time: 1 hour

Filling:	Topping:
1 cup blueberries	1 cup buttermilk baking mix (such as Bisquick)
1 cup cranberries	
1 package frozen raspberries, thawed	½ cup brown sugar
	1 teaspoon cinnamon
½ cup sugar	1 egg, slightly beaten
2 tablespoons all-purpose flour	¼ cup butter or margarine, melted
	Ice cream or frozen yogurt

- ■ Place wire rack into bowl of oven. Preheat oven to 500°F.

- ■ In an 8-inch metal baking pan combine the berries, sugar and flour.

- In a medium bowl combine the baking mix, brown sugar and cinnamon. Add the egg, and mix until mixture is crumbly. Spread over berries. Drizzle with melted butter or margarine. Cover pan with foil, crimping edges to secure. Reduce oven heat to 350°F and bake 35 minutes. Uncover and continue baking 25 minutes or until fruit is tender and topping is golden. Serve warm or at room temperature with ice cream or frozen yogurt.

BANANA PUDDING CUPS

Makes 4

Cooking time: 4 to 5 minutes

3-ounce package vanilla pudding mix
2 cups milk
12 vanilla wafers
1 medium banana cut into 16 slices about ¼-inch thick
12 regular size marshmallows

- Set out four 5 or 6-ounce ovenproof dessert dishes or ramekins.
- Place wire rack into bowl of oven. Preheat oven to 500°F.
- Combine pudding and milk in a medium saucepan. Prepare pudding according to package directions.
- Arrange 3 vanilla wafers in the bottom of each dish. Top wafers with 4 banana slices. Pour an equal amount of pudding over wafers and banana slices in each dish. Place 3 marshmallows on top of each dish. Place dishes in a 9-inch metal baking pan.
- Keep oven heat at 500°F. Bake pudding cups 4 to 5 minutes until marshmallows are golden. Cool slightly before serving. Pudding may also be chilled.

KIDS WILL LOVE BANANA PUDDING CUPS. I KNOW, BECAUSE THEY'RE A HIT AT MY HOUSE. BUT HERE'S A SECRET - MY WIFE AND I LOVE THEM TOO. TRY THEM AT YOUR HOME AND WATCH EVERYONE COME BACK FOR MORE.

MINT TOPPED BROWNIES

Makes 16

Cooking time: 15 minutes

16-ounce box of brownie mix
16 bite-size peppermint patties

- Prepare an 8x8-inch square metal pan according to brownie package directions.
- Place wire rack into bowl of oven. Preheat oven to 500°F.
- Prepare mix according to package directions. Spread batter into pan.
- Reduce oven heat to 325°F. Bake brownies 10 to 12 minutes. Top with patties and continue baking 3 to 5 minutes or until patties are melted. Remove brownies from oven and swirl patties with spatula. Cool and cut into 16 brownies.

SPICY PUMPKIN CUSTARD CUPS

Makes 4

Cooking time: 35 minutes

1 cup canned pumpkin
½ cup sugar
1 egg
1 cup evaporated milk
¾ teaspoon cinnamon

½ teaspoon ground ginger
⅛ teaspoon nutmeg
Pinch of cloves
Pinch of salt
Ice cream or whipping cream

- Grease four 5-ounce custard cups or souffle dishes.
- Place wire rack into bowl of oven. Preheat oven to 500°F.
- In a small mixing bowl combine the pumpkin, sugar, egg, milk, cinnamon, ginger, nutmeg, cloves and salt. Mix well with a wire whisk. Pour pumpkin mixture into cups. Place a 9-inch metal baking pan on bottom rack of oven. Place custard cups in pan. Pour 1-inch boiling water in pan. Place another 9-inch baking pan on top of custard cups as a cover.
- Reduce oven heat to 350°F. Bake custards for 35 minutes or until a knife inserted in center comes out clean. After turning oven off, allow custards to rest in oven for 5 minutes. Serve warm or chilled with ice cream or whipped cream.

Ruth-Ellen's Cinnamon Sugar Cookies

Makes 20 to 25

Cooking time: 5 to 10 minutes

½ cup soft butter or margarine

¾ cup sugar

1 egg

½ teaspoon vanilla

1½ cups all-purpose flour

Pinch salt

1 teaspoon baking powder

2 tablespoons milk

1½ tablespoons sugar

1 tablespoon cinnamon

2 tablespoons softened butter or margarine

■ Grease two 9-inch metal baking pans.

■ Place lower wire rack into bowl of oven. Preheat oven to 500°F.

■ In a large bowl with electric mixer, cream ½ cup butter or margarine with sugar. Add the egg and vanilla. Beat until light and fluffy.

■ In a small bowl blend the flour, salt and baking powder. Add ⅓ of the flour mixture to the butter mixture and beat well. Add the milk then remaining flour. Beat until all the flour is incorporated.

■ In a small bowl combine the sugar and cinnamon for the topping.

■ With floured hands roll small amounts of dough into 1-inch balls. Dip one side of each ball into the cinnamon sugar mixture. Place uncoated side down in pan. Rub softened margarine on the bottom of a small glass, and dip into cinnamon sugar. Press on each cookie with glass to flatten slightly.

■ Reduce oven heat to 350°F. Place one pan on lower rack. Put upper rack in position. Place other pan on upper rack. Bake cookies 5 minutes or until edges are golden. Remove pan from upper rack. Continue baking pan on lower rack for 5 minutes. Cool cookies on wire rack.

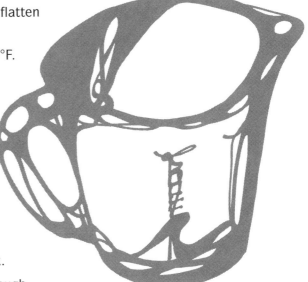

■ Repeat with remaining dough.

PEANUT BUTTER AND MINI-CHIP CUPCAKES WITH PEANUT/CHOCOLATE FROSTING

Makes 12

Cooking time: 15 to 20 minutes

½ of an 18-once yellow cake mix
⅓ cup water
2 eggs
⅓ cup creamy peanut butter
½ cup mini chocolate chips

Frosting:
1 cup creamy peanut butter
1 tablespoon butter or margarine
1 cup powdered sugar
¼ cup unsweetened cocoa powder
½ cup milk

- Fill 12 muffin cups (2 separate pans with 6 cups in each) with paper cupcake liners.

- Place wire rack into bowl of oven. Preheat oven to 500°F.

- With electric mixer blend cake mix, water and eggs. Add peanut butter and beat at medium speed 3 minutes or until well blended. Stir in chips. Fill muffin cups ⅔ full with batter.

- Reduce oven heat to 350°F. Bake 15 to 20 minutes or until a toothpick inserted near the center comes out clean. Remove from oven. Cool on wire rack for 10 minutes, then remove from pan.

- Make frosting: In a small bowl using an electric mixer blend peanut butter and butter or margarine. Blend in sugar and cocoa powder. Add milk, 2 tablespoons at a time, and blend. Beat on high speed until smooth. Frost cupcakes once cooled.

WINTER PLUM COBBLER

Makes 4 Servings

Cooking time: 25 to 30 minutes

1 pound can plums, drained (reserve juice)
1½ cups all-purpose flour
2 teaspoons baking powder
½ teaspoon salt
½ cup sugar

1 egg, well beaten
½ cup milk
½ cup butter or margarine, melted
1 teaspoon cornstarch

- Grease a 9-inch metal baking pan.

- Place wire rack into bowl of oven. Preheat oven to 500°F.

- Arrange drained plums in bottom of baking pan. In a small bowl combine flour, baking powder, salt and sugar. Stir in egg, milk and butter or margarine. Mix gently until all ingredients are blended. Pour over plums.

- Reduce oven to 375°F. Bake cobbler until brown and crusty, about 25 to 30 minutes. Cool on wire rack.

- While cobbler bakes, combine reserved plum syrup and cornstarch. Simmer and stir mixture in a small saucepan until thickened. Serve cobbler warm with sauce.

APPLE CANDY CRISP

Makes 4 Servings

Cooking time: 25 to 30 minutes

3 cups tart apples (such as Granny Smith),
peeled and very thinly sliced

¾ cup all-purpose flour

¾ cup light brown sugar, firmly packed

¼ teaspoon salt

½ teaspoon cinnamon

1 egg yolk, lightly beaten

⅓ cup butter or margarine, melted

- Grease a 9-inch metal baking pan.

- Place wire rack into bowl of oven. Preheat oven to 500°F.

- Place sliced apples in pan in an even layer. In a small bowl blend flour, sugar, salt and cinnamon with a whisk. Add egg yolk and mix until mixture is crumbly. Spread over apples and drizzle with melted butter or margarine.

- Reduce oven heat to 350°F. Bake crisp until apples are tender and top is nicely browned, about 25 minutes. Cool on wire rack. Serve warm or room temperature.

HOLIDAY MINCEMEAT SQUARES WITH LEMON GLAZE

Makes 16

Cooking time: 20 minutes

1 cup all-purpose flour

1½ teaspoons baking powder

½ teaspoon salt

¼ teaspoons vanilla

½ cup butter or margarine

1 cup light brown sugar, firmly packed

1 egg

1 teaspoon vanilla

½ cup prepared mincemeat, drained

½ cup chopped walnuts or pecans

Glaze:

2 tablespoons unsalted butter or margarine, softened

1 cup powdered sugar

1 tablespoon lemon juice

- Grease an 8x8-inch metal baking pan.

- Place wire rack into bowl of oven. Preheat oven to 500°F.

- Combine flour, baking powder and salt.in a small bowl.

- With mixer at medium speed, beat butter or margarine, brown sugar, egg and vanilla in a large bowl until light and fluffy. Stir in mincemeat. Add flour mixture until well combined. Stir in nuts. Place batter in pan.

- Reduce oven heat to 350°F. Bake squares 20 minutes. Cool.

- To make glaze: In small mixer bowl cream butter or margarine and powdered sugar. Add lemon juice, and blend until smooth. Frost and cut squares.

CINNAMON APPLE CAKE

Makes 4 to 6 Servings

Cooking time: 40 to 45 minutes

1½ cups tart apples, peeled and sliced thin

3 tablespoons sugar

1½ teaspoons cinnamon

1⅓ cups all-purpose flour

2 teaspoons baking powder

¼ teaspoon salt

2 eggs

1 cup sugar

½ cup vegetable oil

3 tablespoons apple cider or juice

- Grease an 8x8-inch metal baking pan.
- Place wire rack into bowl of oven. Preheat oven to 500°F.
- In a small bowl top apples with sugar and cinnamon.
- In another bowl blend the flour, baking powder and salt. In a large mixer bowl, beat together the eggs, sugar, vegetable oil, cider and or juice. Add the flour mixture, in thirds, to the egg mixture. Beat well after each addition with a wooden spoon.
- Spoon ⅓ of the batter into the pan. Drain apples of any accumulated liquid. Arrange half the apple slices evenly over the batter. Repeat layering, then top the second layer of apples with remaining batter.
- Reduce oven heat to 350°F. Bake cake 40 to 45 minutes or until top springs back when lightly touched with fingertip. Cool cake thoroughly in pan on wire rack before removing from pan.

ORANGE CREAM CUSTARDS

Makes 4 Servings

Cooking time: 1 hour

1 cup heavy cream	*2 tablespoons sugar*
½ cup milk	*1 teaspoon vanilla extract*
1 egg	*2 teaspoons grated orange rind*
1 egg yolk	

- Grease four 5-ounce ramekins or other ovenproof dishes.
- Place wire rack into bowl of oven. Preheat oven to 500°F.
- In blender or food processor, combine cream, milk, egg, egg yolk, sugar, vanilla and orange rind. Mix well for 30 seconds.
- Pour mixture into ramekins. Put ramekins into a 9-inch metal baking pan. Place in oven. Fill pan to a depth of 1-inch with boiling water. Cover the pan and ramekins with foil or another 9-inch pan.
- Reduce oven heat to 325°F. Bake custards for 1 hour or until knife inserted in center comes out clean. Chill 2 hours. Serve cold.

Maine Blueberry Cake with Blueberry Sauce

Makes 8 Servings

Cooking time: 30 minutes

½ cup butter or margarine

1 cup sugar

1 egg

1½ cups all-purpose flour

1½ teaspoons baking powder

Grated rind of 1 lemon

⅓ cup evaporated milk

1 cup fresh or frozen blueberries

2 tablespoons sugar

½ teaspoon cinnamon

Blueberry Sauce:

1 cup blueberries

⅓ cup sugar

2 teaspoons cornstarch

¼ cup water

- Grease an 8x8-inch square metal baking pan.

- Place wire rack into bowl of oven. Preheat oven to 500°F.

- In a mixing bowl cream butter or margarine and 1 cup sugar. Add egg and beat until combined. In a separate container combine flour, baking powder and rind. Slowly beat into butter mixture. Beat in milk. Fold in blueberries. Turn batter into pan. Combine 2 tablespoons sugar with cinnamon and sprinkle over batter.

- Reduce oven heat to 350°F. Bake cake 30 minutes or until nicely browned and cake tester comes out clean when inserted in center.

- While cake is baking, make sauce. In a small saucepan combine berries and sugar. Dissolve cornstarch in water and add to berries. Cook, stirring constantly, over medium heat until clear and thickened.

Cherry Almond Tarts

Makes 3 Tarts

Cooking time: 15 minutes

1 sheet prepared pie crust dough

30-ounce can cherry pie filling

½ teaspoon almond extract

3 teaspoons butter or margarine, melted

- Place wire rack into bowl of oven. Preheat oven to 500°F.

- Prepare pie crust, line pans, and pre-bake tart shells as described in Chocolate Pecan Tarts below.

- In a small bowl thoroughly mix cherry pie filling, almond extract and melted butter or margarine.

- With tart pans still in the oven, carefully fill each tart shell with ⅓ of the filling.

- Reduce oven heat to 350°F. Bake tarts 10 minutes or until crusts are nicely browned and filling begins to bubble. Cool on wire rack. Serve warm or room temperature.

CHOCOLATE PECAN TARTS

Makes 3

Cooking time: 19 minutes

¾ cup chopped pecans
½ cup chocolate chips
⅓ cup sugar
½ cup dark corn syrup
1 teaspoon vanilla

1 tablespoon butter or margarine, melted
1 large egg, beaten
1 sheet prepared pie crust dough

- Set out three 4½-inch tart pans.

- Place wire rack into bowl of oven. Preheat oven to 500°F.

- In a medium bowl mix together the pecans and chips. In another medium bowl whisk together the sugar, corn syrup, vanilla, butter or margarine and egg.

- Place pie dough on a floured work surface. Turn a 4½-inch tart pan upside down on the pie dough. Cut 3 circles of dough ½-inch larger then the circumference of the tart pan. Line each pan with a circle of dough. Crimp edges. Use dough scraps if necessary to patch any areas. Press dough to edge of pan with tines of a fork. Prick dough all over with tines of fork.

- Reduce oven heat to 425°F. Bake pie crust 4 minutes or until golden. Remove from oven. Distribute nut and chip mixture evenly among the three pans. Pour corn syrup mixture evenly over nuts and chips. Return pans to oven and bake 4 to 5 minutes. Be careful not to let tarts burn. Reduce oven heat to 350°F. Cover tarts with a 9-inch baking pan right side up. Bake 10 minutes. Cool on wire rack. Serve at room temperature with ice cream.

ULTIMATE CHIP COOKIES

Makes 24

Cooking time: 5 to 10 minutes

½ cup butter or margarine

½ cup brown sugar, firmly packed

½ cup white sugar

1 egg

1 teaspoon vanilla

1 cup all-purpose flour

1¼ cups old-fashioned oatmeal

½ teaspoon salt

½ teaspoon baking soda

½ teaspoon baking powder

½ cup mini-chocolate chips

½ cup vanilla chips

½ cup walnuts, chopped coarsely

½ cup raisins

- Grease two 9-inch metal baking pans.

- Place wire rack into bowl of oven. Preheat oven to 500°F.

- In a large bowl with electric mixer, cream butter or margarine and sugars. Beat in the egg until mixture is light and fluffy. Mix in vanilla.

- In a small bowl blend the flour, oatmeal, salt, baking soda and baking powder.

- Add the flour mixture to the butter or margarine mixture in three batches, beating after each addition. When all the flour is incorporated, mix in the mini chips, vanilla chips, nuts and raisins. Mix well to distribute ingredients evenly.

- Drop dough by spoonfuls in mounds no larger than 1-inch in diameter. With floured fingertips, slightly flatten the cookies that will bake on the upper rack. Make 6 mounds per pan.

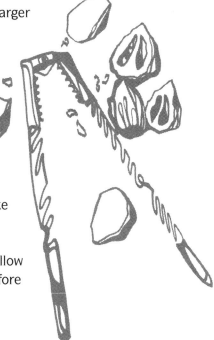

- Reduce oven heat to 350°F. Place a pan of cookies on the bottom rack. Put upper rack in position. Place the pan of flattened cookies on the upper rack. Bake cookies 5 minutes or until edges are golden. Remove pan from upper rack. Continue baking lower rack 5 minutes. Allow cookies to cool in pan 2 to 3 minutes before removing. Cool on a wire rack.

- Repeat with remaining dough.

JULIE'S CHOCOLATE ALLIGATOR COOKIES

Makes 24 Cookies

Cooking time: 6 to 12 minutes

½ cup butter or margarine	¼ cup unsweetened cocoa
1 cup sugar	Pinch salt
1 egg	1 teaspoon baking powder
½ teaspoon vanilla	3 tablespoons milk
1¼ cups all-purpose flour	½ powdered sugar

- Grease two 9-inch metal baking pans.

- In a large bowl with electric mixer, cream butter or margarine and sugar. Beat in the egg and vanilla until mixture is light and fluffy.

- In a small bowl blend the flour, cocoa, salt and baking powder. Add ⅓ of the flour mixture to the butter or margarine mixture, beating well. Beat in the milk and remaining flour mixture. Place the mixture in the refrigerator to chill for 1 hour.

- Place lower wire rack into bowl of oven. Preheat oven to 500°F.

- Place powdered sugar on a small plate. Remove dough from refrigerator. With floured hands, roll dough into 1-inch balls. Roll each ball in powdered sugar to coat.

- Place 6 balls in each pan. Flatten cookies slightly with floured fingertips.

- Reduce oven heat to 350°F. Place a pan of cookies on bottom rack. Put upper rack in position. Place a second pan of cookies on upper rack. Bake for 6 minutes or until edges are lightly browned.

- Remove pan from upper rack. Continue baking lower rack for another 6 minutes. Cool cookies on wire rack.

- Repeat with remaining dough.

*T*HE ENTIRE WORLD LOVES CHOCOLATE. THERE REALLY IS NO SUBSTITUTE. CHOCOLATE IS SO MUCH A PART OF TODAY'S DESSERTS. TRY THESE DECADENT RECIPES FOR YOUR FAMILY OR FRIENDS. THEY WON'T BE DISAPPOINTED.

Hermit Bars

Cooking time: 20 minutes

½ cup butter or margarine

1 cup firmly packed brown sugar

1 egg

½ cup sour cream

1½ cups all-purpose flour

½ teaspoon salt

1 teaspoon cinnamon

¼ teaspoon cloves

½ teaspoon ground ginger

1 cup chopped walnuts

1 cup raisins

- Grease an 8x8-inch metal baking pan.

- Place wire rack into bowl of oven. Preheat oven to 500°F.

- In a mixer bowl cream the butter or margarine and sugar. Beat in the egg and sour cream. Add the flour, salt, cinnamon, cloves and ginger. Stir by hand to combine. Add the nuts and raisins, mixing gently. Turn batter into pan.

- Reduce oven heat to 350°F. Bake 20 minutes or until surface of hermit bars is springy to the touch. Cut into bars.

Raisin Cookies

Makes 24 to 30

Cooking time: 5 to 10 minutes

¼ cup butter or margarine

½ cup sugar

1 egg

1 teaspoon vanilla

1¼ cups all-purpose flour

¼ teaspoon baking soda

1½ tablespoons sour cream

¼ cup raisins

Pinch salt

- Grease two 9-inch metal baking pans.

- Place lower wire rack into bowl of oven. Preheat oven to 500°F.

- In a large bowl with electric mixer, cream butter or margarine and sugar. Add egg and beat until fluffy. Add vanilla.

- In a small bowl blend the flour and baking soda. Add ⅓ of the flour to the butter mixture. Add the sour cream and mix until blended. Add remaining flour, and mix until all flour is incorporated. Stir in raisins.

- Drop dough from a spoon in mounds about 1-inch in diameter. You will need to push dough from the spoon with your finger - it's very stiff. Place 6 mounds in each pan. Flatten cookies slightly with floured fingertips. Place one pan on the lower rack of oven. Put the upper rack in position, place second pan on upper rack.

- Reduce oven heat to 350°F. Bake cookies 5 minutes or until edges are golden. Remove pan from upper rack. Continue baking lower rack for 5 minutes. Cool cookies on wire rack.

- Repeat with remaining dough.

POT-DE-CREME KAHLUA

Makes 4 Servings

Cooking time: 1 hour

½ cup milk	2 tablespoons sugar
½ cup semi-sweet chocolate chips	2 tablespoons Kahlua or other coffee liqueur
1 cup heavy cream	
2 eggs	Whipped cream

- Grease four 5 ounce souffle dishes.

- Place wire rack into bowl of oven. Preheat oven to 500°F.

- Heat milk to boiling. In food processor or blender, chop chocolate chips until fine. With motor running pour in hot milk, and process until smooth. Add heavy cream, eggs, sugar and Kahlua. Pour into souffle dishes.

- Reduce oven heat to 325°F. Place a 9-inch metal baking pan on wire rack. Place souffle dishes in pan. Pour 1-inch of boiling water into the pan around the souffle dishes. Cover pan with foil or another 9-inch baking pan. Bake 1 hour or until knife inserted in center comes out clean. Let rest in oven 5 minutes. Chill. Serve with whipped cream.

PEAR AND CRANBERRY CRUMBLE

Makes 4 Servings

Cooking time: 30 to 35 minutes

16-ounce can pear halves, drained and sliced

½ cup cranberries

1 tablespoon orange juice

½ cup firmly packed light brown sugar

¼ cup butter or margarine

½ cup all-purpose flour

- Grease an 8x8-inch metal baking pan.

- Place wire rack into bowl of oven. Preheat oven to 500°F.

- Spread the pears and cranberries in the bottom of the pan. Sprinkle with orange juice and 3 tablespoons of the brown sugar.

- In a small bowl blend together the remaining brown sugar, butter or margarine and flour until the mixture resembles coarse meal. Sprinkle the fruits with the flour mixture.

- Reduce oven heat to 350°F. Bake the crumble for 30 to 35 minutes or until golden. Cool on wire rack 10 minutes. Serve warm.

BETH'S QUICK LEMON ALMOND POUND CAKE

Makes 1 Loaf

Cooking time: 60 minutes

16-ounce packaged pound cake mix

2 eggs

6-ounce container lemon flavored yogurt

½ teaspoon almond extract

Grated rind of one lemon

2 tablespoons milk

- Grease a 9x5-inch loaf pan.

- Place wire rack into bowl of oven. Preheat oven to 500°F.

- In a mixer bowl, combine cake mix, eggs, yogurt, extract, rind and milk. Beat 1 minute on low speed, then 2 minutes on high. Pour batter into loaf pan.

- Reduce oven heat to 325°F. Bake cake 60 minutes or until cake tester inserted in center of cake comes out clean. Allow to cool in pan 10 minutes. Turn out onto wire rack to cool completely. The top of the cake will crack, this is a normal occurrence in this cake.

QUICK PEACH AND RASPBERRY COBBLER

Makes 4 Servings

Cooking time: 30 minutes

*16-ounce can peach slices
(preferably in own juice), drained*

*¾ cup frozen raspberries, thawed
and drained*

3 tablespoons brown sugar

*½ of an 18½-ounce box yellow
cake mix*

1 egg

⅓ cup water

¼ cup vegetable oil

Vanilla ice cream

- Grease a 9-inch metal baking pan.

- Place wire rack into bowl of oven. Preheat oven to 500°F.

- Spread peach slices and raspberries in the bottom of the pan. Toss with the brown sugar.

- In a small bowl combine cake mix, egg, water and oil. Mix with a wire whisk or wooden spoon until well blended. Pour batter over fruit.

- Reduce oven heat to 350°F. Bake cobbler 30 minutes or until cake tester comes out clean when inserted near center. Cool on wire rack 10 minutes. Serve warm with vanilla ice cream.

S'MORES INDOORS

Makes 6

Cooking time: 2 minutes

6 graham crackers, broken in half

3 chocolate bars, 1½ ounces each

6 marshmallows

- Place upper rack in bowl of oven. Preheat oven to 500°F.

- Reduce oven heat to 450°F. Lay 6 graham cracker halves on upper rack of oven. Top each with a marshmallow. Bake until marshmallow is puffed and golden - about 1 minute. Top each marshmallow with ½ of a chocolate bar. Continue baking until chocolate begins to melt - about 1 minute. Remove from oven and top each with another graham cracker half. Press together, serve warm.

INDEX

Cajun Shrimp, 110
Cakes
    Mini Southern Crab Cakes with
        Caper Tartar Sauce, 29
    Roasted Crab Cakes, 111
Cape Cod Cranberry Whole
    Wheat Muffins, 44
Caribbean Chicken Diablo, 78
Carrots
    Baby Carrots in Lemon
        Mint Glaze, 129
    Baked Kielbasa with Red Peppers
        and Carrots, 168
Casseroles
    Creamy Ravioli Casserole, 140
    Ham and Cheese Souffleed
        Casserole with Corn Muffins, 162
Cauliflower in Mustard
    Cream Sauce, 126
    Black Olives and Capers, 132
Celery
    Pearl Onions Baked in
        Celery Sauce, 125
    Roasted Fennel and Celery, 119
Cheese
    Artichoke and Scallion Gratin, 24
    Bacon Tomato and
        Cheese Turnovers, 26
    Baked Chilies Rellenos, 166
    Baked Penne with Fontina
        and Pesto, 141
    Baked Shells and Cheese with
        Sun-Dried Tomatoes and Fresh-
        Baked Sesame Rolls, 160
    Baked Stuffed Potatoes with
        Herb Cheese, 130
    Boneless Pork Chops with
        Orange Dijon Parmesan Crust, 86
    Coffee Buns, 59
    Crab and Brie Tostadas with
        Fresh Cranberry Salsa, 34
    Creamy Spinach Gratin, 126
    Crostini with Pepperoni
        and Provolone, 34
    Dried Beef and Onion Dip, 28
    Fennel Baked Cod with Tomatoes
        and Feta Cheese, 154
    Fontina and Prosciutto Lasagna with
        Hot Poppy Seed Bread, 157
    Grecian Zucchini, 121
    Ham and Cheese Biscuits with
        Mustard Mayo, 24
    Ham and Cheese Sandwiches
        Italian Style, 144
    Ham and Cheese Souffleed
        Casserole with Corn Muffins, 162

Herb Crusted Zucchini, 120
Hot Mexicana Dip, 32
Jalapeno Corn Muffins, 72
Mexican Pizza with
    Cornmeal Crust, 71
Mexican Turkey Burgers with Easy
    Cheesy Potatoes, 148
Mini Meat Loaves with Quick
    Zucchini Parmesan, 163
Mini Open Face Reubens, 22
Nachos Supreme, 23
Pepper Boats with Rice and
    Black Beans, 120
Pizza Primavera, 70
Pork Tenderloin Rolls Stuffed with
    Cheese and Chilies, 86
Puffed Provolone Custard, 145
Rolled Boneless Turkey Breast with
    Pepperoni and Mozzarella, 83
Shrimp and Fontina Pizza, 152
Tomato, Bacon and Two
    Cheese Strata, 149
Tortellini Broccoli Bake with
    Herb Garlic Toast, 156
Tortilla Pizza with Cheese, Chilies
    and Enchilada Sauce, 28
Tuna Melt with Tomatoes
    and Capers, 143
Turkey Enchiladas with
    Spicy Black Beans, 153
Veal Chops Stuffed with
    Spinach and Three Cheeses, 89
Veggie Wedgies, 36
Whole Wheat Pizza with
    Capocollo and Two Cheeses, 70
Cherry Almond Tarts, 184
Chicken
    Caribbean Chicken Diablo, 78
    Easy Cassoulet, 146
    Hot and Smoky Chicken Wings, 22
    Oven Fried Chicken with
        Southwest Spices, 79
    Roasted Chicken Nicoise, 80
    Sesame Scallion Chicken Bites, 25
    Tandoori Skewers with
        Herbed Pitas, 159
Chives
    Baked Stuffed Tomatoes with
        Mushrooms and Chives, 124
    Bluefish Fillets with Lemon
        Chive Caper Sauce, 107
    Seafood with Dill Chive
        Butter Sauce, 99
    Tiny Herb Biscuits with Chive
        Spread and Roast Beef, 33

Beth's Quick Lemon Almond
  Pound Cake, 190
Bluefish Fillets with Lemon Chive
  Caper Sauce, 107
Cornish Hens with Lemon
  and Herbs, 81
Holiday Mincemeat Squares with
  Lemon Glaze, 182
Lamb Marinated in Thyme
  and Lemon, 92
Pepper Potatoes, 129
Rice Stuffed Grape Leaves, 35
Saucy Lemon Cake Cups, 174
Scallops with Quick Rouille, 112
Lobster
  Seafood with Dill Chive
    Butter Sauce, 99
Louisiana Breakfast Puffs, 58

Maine Blueberry Cake with
  Blueberry Sauce, 184
Meat & Poultry
  Beef
  Peppered Beef Fillet, 84
  Ragin' Cajun Meat Loaf, 85
  Wine Braised Brisket, 84
  Chicken
  Caribbean Chicken Diablo, 78
  Cornish Hens with Lemon
    and Herbs, 81
  Oven Fried Chicken with
    Southwest Spices, 79
  Roasted Chicken Nicoise, 80
  Thai Spiced Cornish Hens, 78
  Lamb
  Grilled Rib Lamb Chops with
    Wilted Greens, 91
  Lamb Marinated in Thyme
    and Lemon, 92
  Loin Lamb Chops with Tomatoes
    and Onions, 92
  Pork
  Boneless Pork Chops with Orange
    Dijon Parmesan Crust, 86
  Ham and Pineapple Kabobs with
    Chutney Curry Glaze, 89
  Pork Tenderloin Rolls Stuffed with
    Cheese and Chilies, 86
  Spicy Pork Sate, 88
  Tequila Lime Pork Tenderloin with
    Enchilada Cream Sauce, 87
  Turkey
  Boneless Turkey Breast with Pesto
    and Balsamic Vinegar, 82
  Rolled Boneless Turkey Breast with
    Pepperoni and Mozzarella, 83

Savory Confetti Turkey Loaf, 82
  Veal
  Roasted Veal Loin with Garlic
    and Thyme, 90
  Veal Chops in Orange
    Basil Sauce, 90
  Veal Chops Stuffed with Spinach
    and Three Cheeses, 89
Meat Loaf
  Mini Meat Loaves with Quick
    Zucchini Parmesan, 163
Mexican Pizza with Cornmeal Crust, 71
Mexican Turkey Burgers with Easy
  Cheesy Potatoes, 148
Mid-West Harvest Bread, 46
Mini Meat Loaves with Quick
  Zucchini Parmesan, 163
Mini Open Face Reubens, 22
Mini Southern Crab Cakes with Caper
  Tartar Sauce, 29
Mint Topped Brownies, 178
Monkfish
  Grilled Monkfish with Mustard
    Parsley Sauce, 105
  Roasted Monkfish with Onions,
    Herbs and Spices, 106
Muffins
  Baked Turkey Sausage and Eggs
    with Honey English Muffins, 139
  Blueberry Muffins with Nutmeg, 52
  Cape Cod Cranberry Whole
    Wheat Muffins, 44
  Easy Pecan Pumpkin Muffins, 45
  Ham and Cheese Souffleed
    Casserole with Corn Muffins, 162
  Jalapeno Corn Muffins, 72
  Spicy Sweet Potato Muffins, 68
Mushrooms
  Baked Stuffed Tomatoes with
    Mushrooms and Chives, 124
  Flounder with Shiitake Mushrooms
    and Black Beans, 102
  Surprise Stuffed Mushrooms, 27

Nachos Supreme, 23
New Potatoes with Parsley Butter, 128

Oatmeal Raisin Walnut Bread, 67
Old-Fashioned Popovers, 53
Olive Biscuits, 51
Onions
  Artichoke and Scallion Gratin, 24
  Baked Frittata with Gold Potatoes,
    Red Onions and Black Caviar, 31
  Dark Onion Rye, 52

Dried Beef and Onion Dip, 28
Grilled Italian Sausage with
Red Onions, 146
Loin Lamb Chops with Tomatoes
and Onions, 92
Pearl Onions Baked in
Celery Sauce, 125
Roasted Monkfish with Onions,
Herbs and Spices, 106
Sesame Scallion Chicken Bites, 25
Orange
Cream Custards, 183
Raisin Scones, 61
Oven Fried Chicken with
Southwest Spices, 79

Peanut Butter and Mini-Chip Cupcakes
with Peanut/Chocolate Frosting, 180
Pear and Cranberry Crumble, 190
Pearl Onions Baked in
Celery Sauce, 125
Pecan
Chocolate Pecan Tarts, 185
Crusted Snapper Fillets with
Lime Butter, 100
Easy Pecan Pumpkin Muffins, 45
Peppercorns
Lemon Pepper Potatoes, 129
Peppered Beef Fillet, 84
Tuscan Black Pepper Bread, 48
Peppers
Baked Kielbasa with Red Peppers
and Carrots, 168
Broccoli, Corn and Peppers with
Lime Butter, 127
Pepper Boats with Rice and
Black Beans, 120
Peppers Provencal, 32
Roasted Peppers, Potatoes and
Green Beans, 131
Swordfish with Sun-Dried Tomatoes
and Roasted Yellow Peppers, 103
Zippy Corn and Red
Pepper Timbales, 130
Philadelphia Butter Cake, 65
Pizza
Easy Pizza Dough, 69
Mexican Pizza with
Cornmeal Crust, 71
Primavera, 70
Shrimp and Fontina Pizza, 152
Tortilla Pizza with Cheese, Chilies
and Enchilada Sauce, 28
Whole Wheat Pizza with Capocollo
and Two Cheeses, 70

Pork
Boneless Pork Chops with Orange
Dijon Parmesan Crust, 86
Grilled Italian Sausage with
Red Onions, 146
Ham and Cheese Biscuits with
Mustard Mayo, 24
Ham and Cheese Souffleed
Casserole with Corn Muffins, 162
Ham and Pineapple Kebabs with
Chutney Curry Glaze, 89
Savory Ham Patties and Baby Corn
With Chili Butter, 161
Spicy Pork Sate, 88
Tenderloin Rolls Stuffed with Cheese
and Chilies, 86
Tequila Lime Pork Tenderloin with
Enchilada Cream Sauce, 87
Pot-de-Creme Kahlua, 189
Potatoes
Baked Acorn Squash with Sweet
Potatoes and Golden Raisins, 123
Baked Frittata with Gold Potatoes,
Red Onions, and Black Caviar, 31
Baked Stuffed Potatoes with
Herb Cheese, 130
Hot Corned Beef Special Pockets
with German Potato Salad, 167
Lemon Pepper Potatoes, 129
Mexican Turkey Burgers with Easy
Cheesy Potatoes, 148
New Potatoes with
Parsley Butter, 128
Roasted Chicken Nicoise, 80
Roasted New Potato and Beet
Salad with Dill Dressing, 118
Roasted Peppers, Potatoes and
Green Beans, 131
Smoked Honey Mustard Pork
Chops with Baked Sweet
Potato Rounds, 158
Spicy Sweet Potato Muffins, 68
Tiny New Potatoes with
Smoked Salmon, 30
Puffed Provolone Custard, 145
Puffy Pear Pancake, 151
Pumpkin
Easy Pecan Pumpkin Muffins, 45
Spicy Pumpkin Custard Cups, 178

Quick and Complete Meals
Baked Chilies Rellenos, 166
Baked Kielbasa with Red Peppers
and Carrots, 168
Baked Penne with Fontina
and Pesto, 141

Baked Shells and Cheese with Sun-Dried Tomatoes and Fresh-Baked Sesame Rolls, 160

Baked Turkey Sausage and Eggs with Honey English Muffins, 139

BLT Pizza, 164

Chicken Tandoori Skewers with Herbed Pitas, 159

Creamy Ravioli Casserole, 140

Easy Cassoulet, 146

Eggs Benedict from The Oven with Quick Hollandaise, 144

Fajita Fillets with Tex-Mex Macaroni Medley, 165

Fennel Baked Cod with Tomatoes and Feta Cheese, 154

Fontina and Prosciutto Lasagna with Hot Poppy Seed Bread, 157

Giant Orange Scented Bacon Popover, 150

Grilled Italian Sausage with Red Onions, 146

Ham and Cheese Sandwiches Italian Style, 144

Ham and Cheese Souffleed Casserole with Corn Muffins, 162

Hot Corned Beef Special Pockets with German Potato Salad, 167

Mexican Turkey Burgers with Easy Cheesy Potatoes, 148

Mini Meat Loaves with Quick Zucchini Parmesan, 163

Puffed Provolone Custard, 145

Puffy Pear Pancake, 151

Roast Beef Melt with Horseradish Sauce and Zesty French Fries, 166

Roasted Tuna with Grilled Vegetables, 147

Savory Ham Patties and Baby Corn With Chili Butter, 161

Shrimp and Fontina Pizza, 152

Shrimp Orzo and Artichoke Bake, 142

Smoked Honey Mustard Pork Chops with Baked Sweet Potato Rounds, 158

Sweet and Sour Turkey Stuffed Cabbage Rolls, 138

Tomato, Bacon and Two Cheese Strata, 149

Tortellini Broccoli Bake with Herb Garlic Toast, 156

Tuna Melt with Tomatoes and Capers, 143

Turkey Enchiladas with Spicy Black Beans, 153

Western Bean Bake and Hot Rolls, 155

Quick Peach and Raspberry Cobbler, 191

Ragin' Cajun Meat Loaf, 85

Raisin Cookies, 188

Red Snapper Fillets with Olives, 108

Roast Beef Melt with Horseradish Sauce and Zesty French Fries, 166

Roasted
  Brussels Sprouts, 132
  Chicken Nicoise, 80
  Crab Cakes, 111
  Fennel and Celery, 119
  Monkfish with Onions, Herbs and Spices, 106
  New Potato and Beet Salad with Dill Dressing, 118
  Peppers, Potatoes and Green Beans, 131
  Roasted Chicken Nicoise, 80
  Tuna with Grilled Vegetables, 147
  Veal Loin with Garlic and Thyme, 90

Rolled Boneless Turkey Breast with Pepperoni and Mozzarella, 83

Rosemary and Sun-Dried Tomato Focaccia, 47

Ruth-Ellen's Cinnamon Sugar Cookies, 179

Salmon
  and Swordfish Nuggets in Grapefruit Butter, 110
  Fillets in Tomato Caper Sauce, 104
  Seafood with Dill Chive Butter Sauce, 99
  Steaks with Mustard Dill Sauce, 101
  Tiny New Potatoes with Smoked Salmon, 30

Sandwiches
  Ham and Cheese Sandwiches Italian Style, 144
  Mini Open Face Reubens, 22

Saucy Lemon Cake Cups, 174

Sausage
  Baked Kielbasa with Red Peppers and Carrots, 168
  Baked Turkey Sausage and Eggs with Honey English Muffins, 139
  Crostini with Pepperoni and Provolone, 34
  Grilled Italian Sausage with Red Onions, 146

Savory Confetti Turkey Loaf, 82
Savory Ham Patties and Baby Corn
   with Chili Butter, 161
Scallops
   Basil Garlic Shrimp and Scallops
      en Brochette, 111
   Grilled Sea Scallops in Cranberry
      Grapefruit Sauce, 112
   Lemon Scallops with
      Quick Rouille, 112
   Seafood with Dill Chive
      Butter Sauce, 99
   Surprise Stuffed Mushrooms, 27
Seafood with Dill Chive
   Butter Sauce, 99
Sesame Scallion Chicken Bites, 25
Shrimp
   and Fontina Pizza, 152
   Basil Garlic Shrimp and Scallops
      en Brochette, 111
   Cajun Shrimp, 110
   Orzo and Artichoke Bake, 142
   Seafood with Dill Chive
      Butter Sauce, 99
Smoked Honey Mustard Pork
   Chops with Baked Sweet
   Potato Rounds, 158
S'mores Indoors, 191
Snapper
   in Tarragon Lime Sauce, 102
   Pecan Crusted Snapper Fillets with
      Lime Butter, 100
   Red Snapper Fillets with Olives, 108
Soft Pretzels, 54
Sour Cream
   Artichoke and Scallion Gratin, 24
   Baked Frittata with Gold Potatoes,
      Red Onions and Black Caviar, 31
   Baked Stuffed Potatoes with
      Herb Cheese, 130
   Cauliflower in Mustard
      Cream Sauce, 126
   Cheesy Coffee Buns, 59
   Coffee Cake, 63
   Easy Raspberry Coffee Cake, 60
   Gingerbread, 176
   Nachos Supreme, 23
   Pecan Crusted Snapper Fillets with
      Lime Butter, 100
   Southern Sour Cream Biscuits, 50
   Tequila Lime Pork Tenderloin with
      Enchilada Cream Sauce, 87
   Tiny New Potatoes with
      Smoked Salmon, 30
   Turkey Enchiladas with Spicy
      Black Beans, 153

Southern Sour Cream Biscuits, 50
Spinach
   Basil Turnovers, 30
   Creamy Spinach Gratin, 126
   Veal Chops Stuffed with Spinach
      and Three Cheeses, 89
Spicy Pork Sate, 88
Spicy Pumpkin Custard Cups, 178
Spicy Sweet Potato Muffins, 68
Spinach Basil Turnovers, 30
Squash
   Baked Acorn Squash with Sweet
      Potatoes and Golden Raisins, 123
Summer Vegetable Torte with Pesto
   and Raspberry Vinaigrette, 122
Surprise Stuffed Mushrooms, 27
Sweet and Sour Braised
   Red Cabbage, 128
Sweet and Sour Turkey Stuffed
   Cabbage Rolls, 138
Swordfish
   Baked Tuna or Swordfish with White
      Beans and Garlic, 106
   Salmon and Swordfish Nuggets in
      Grapefruit Butter, 110
   with Sun-Dried Tomatoes and
      Roasted Yellow Peppers, 103

Tarts
   Cherry Almond Tarts, 184
   Chocolate Pecan Tarts, 185
Tequila Lime Pork Tenderloin with
   Enchilada Cream Sauce, 87
Thai Spiced Cornish Hens, 78
Three Berry Crumble, 176
Tiny Herb Biscuits with Chive Spread
   and Roast Beef, 33
Tiny New Potatoes with
   Smoked Salmon, 30
Tomatoes
   Bacon and Two Cheese Strata, 149
   Bacon Tomato and
      Cheese Turnovers, 26
   Baked Shells and Cheese with Sun-
      Dried Tomatoes and Fresh-Baked
      Sesame Rolls, 160
   Baked Stuffed Tomatoes with
      Mushrooms and Chives, 124
   Broiled Cod Fillets with Tomato
      Butter Sauce, 108
   Fennel Baked Cod with Tomatoes
      and Feta Cheese, 154
   Loin Lamb Chops with Tomatoes
      and Onions, 92
   Rosemary and Sun-Dried
      Tomato Focaccia, 47